Also in the **YORKIE BOYS** series...

ISBN 9781912639786

http://getbook.at/YB

ISBN 9781913653620

http://getbook.at/YBAG

YORKIE BOYS

GO FISHING

To Denise

Hope you enjoy the Irish scenes!

David Clough

DAVID CLOUGH

This edition first published in paperback by
Michael Terence Publishing in 2022
www.mtp.agency

ISBN 9781800943551

Cover image
by courtesy of David Clough

Contents

Part One

Part Two

Part One

My fishing credentials

My own credentials as a fisherman are simply a whole lifetime of wonderful fishing experiences.

I have failed to catch fish in many of the great fishing waters of the world. I went salmon fishing on the Spey and caught a seagull. I trolled for sharks in Portugal and caught dysentery from my luncheon meat sandwiches. I spearfished for barracuda off Grand Bahama and shot my fishing partner, a previously mild-mannered Barbadian called Alwyn, who still bears me a grudge and the scar I gave him.

I claim no special expertise. My only claim to fame is that when I fail to catch anything, as I usually do, I remain philosophical about the defeat at the hands (fins?) of my fishy foes. And recently I've even stopped hurling rocks at them in frustration.

I possess no wonderful tackle and have no intention of ever buying any of the fantastic gadgets that are now on the market. I am content to drool over them in tackle shop windows, and wonder whether these massive wagglers and donglers are aids to catching fish or to undreamed-of heights of sexual arousal.

I've never even caught any exceptional fish, apart from one described later in this book – so if you want a bookful of monsters go and buy one by that bloke on television who is always catching them. He has only to sit down next to a river and the bloody fish spring out at him and land on his lap.

Sometimes I catch fish, more often I catch nothing at all – but the point is that it doesn't matter to me whether I catch fish or not. If I don't get anything, it teaches me to appreciate those times when I do catch fish. To catch too many or too easily sickens the spirit. A glut quickly becomes a bore and no-one respects a pushover, whether it is in fishing, or in everyday life.

I'm sure I think more of that one measly hard-faced old trout I fought a day to catch, wading miles over rocks, stumbling, starving and soaking myself to find it, than half a dozen fat factory fish with flesh like sponges. I'd rather there was no rise at all, than a rise in response to a handful of food pellets.

These fishing tales are all mine, so if my any mischance I have given offence to some miserable misbegotten creature who has crossed me in the past, well that's highly regrettable, but sadly for you, not highly remunerative. If any of you have any bright ideas about suing me – forget it lads – I've put everything in the wife's name. You can forget your dreams of fame and fortune at my expense.

I am at present a homeless itinerant, surviving only on my Benefit payments and the good wishes of our wonderful government. I spend my days happily fishing without a care in the world.

All correspondence to me is therefore:

c/o the layby,
just off the road to Lough Erne,
Co. Fermanagh

In the beginning

My fishing story began many years ago, long before I was born, with my great Grandad Benjamin Clough. Old Ben was originally a horse dealer in Leeds, but because the locals kept stealing his horses, he moved out to a little village in Nidderdale called Hampsthwaite, where the locals were less predatory. Hampsthwaite is an ancient village by the river Nidd, a village where Ben became a farmer and his horses were left in peace.

Ben farmed the flat and fertile fields beside the churchyard of St. Thomas a Becket and alongside the River Nidd, which ambled its way through Nidderdale towards Killinghall, the next village downstream. The old church is both interesting and historic, the name Thomas a Becket coming from Hugh de Morville, the leader of the knights who murdered Thomas.

Hugh had expected his king, Henry II, to reward him handsomely for this service. Instead, Henry bitterly regretted the murder and blamed Hugh and his pals for getting him bad publicity. Too late for poor Thomas however, and for Hugh de Morville. He and his three fellow murderers fled to Yorkshire, hiding themselves away in the formidable fortress of Knaresborough Castle. The good citizens of the town wanted nothing to do with such miscreants, so the murderers were rightly shunned as criminals. As a result de Morville was stricken by a guilty conscience and in a vain attempt at contrition, had the church built in nearby Hampsthwaite and named after his victim, as an act of penance.

Old Ben Clough must have been an energetic character as he managed to combine farming, breeding horses, and running a horse dealership as well as the local pub, the Joiners Arms. By his industry he made enough money to build in the village an extensive farm, a terrace of stone houses, the Methodist Chapel, and other houses scattered around the Dale. However, Old Ben can't have been busy making money all the time, because he sired eighteen children, thereby doing his bit to stop the depopulation of the Dales. Among these children was my grandad, George Henry.

My Yorkshire Grandad George Henry was a legendary fisherman, an original stalwart of the local angling club on the Nidd, sometime in the 1890s. It was said of him that he could catch fish on the Nidd when no-one else could, and this was in the days when all the fish were crafty wild fish, not the gullible pellet-fed farm fish of today.

George Henry had been a soldier throughout the First World War, in the Machine Gun Corps (Heavy Section.) The MGCHS recruited only the fittest and most intelligent young soldiers to man the guns inside the newest invention of war, the tank. He was inside this infernal machine at the very first tank battles of Flers, then Cambrai, Arras and Third Ypres. The noise, the heat of the engine, the smoke, the shelling, the likelihood of burning to death made life inside a tank absolutely hellish (and usually, very short.) The casualty rate among these tank crews was horrific. It was a nightmare experience.

Unlike most of his colleagues in the MGCHS, George Henry somehow survived the war, but it had left him a quiet, taciturn man, a man who would rather be gardening on his own in his beloved orchard, or best of all, fishing in the River Nidd.

When I was a little boy he used to take me to his orchard on Crag Top Knaresborough, and let me happily potter about all day, eating plums and pears and having fights with Kaiser Bill, the aggressive billygoat he kept there. Later memories of him after the orchard was sold are of an old man with red cheeks and white eyes. He used to sit in his cottage all day, in a short-sleeved cardigan and a collarless shirt, waiting to be taken to the river, because by then he was completely blind.

He may have had the staring white eyes, which so fascinated and frightened us children, but unbelievably he was still able to catch fish. As long as he was led to the bank he could still pull out trout, even when everyone else failed.

He was primarily a fly fisherman, though when his sight had gone completely he had to resort to the worms. He used greenheart rods and heavy brassbound wooden reels, ancient tackle which he regarded with affection.

Recently I saw a brassbound wooden reel just like the ones Grandad used, on sale in an Antique Fair. Seeing it took me straight back that darkened room in his cottage and the smell of varnish and the old man sitting there silently waiting for his friend Dr Watson to come and take him to the river. The reel was for sale at £200, which would surely have brought a smile even to Grandad's sad old face.

He died before I was old enough to take him fishing, so I gained little from him except his name and a desire to be a skilful fisherman in my own right.

Grandad's tackle and club membership passed down to my uncle, my father being too interested in electronics to learn the skills of fishing. My uncle inherited Grandad's membership of the club, his houseful of antique tackle and some, though not all, of his ability.

As an upstream wormer, there were few to match Uncle George, but of the fly and the nymph he knew nothing – an unfortunate omission in my opinion.

Nevertheless, and to his credit, he still used the old brass and wood spinning reels passed down from his father. There must be easier ways of catching trout than using such antique gear, but he persevered with the ancient tackle. I think I know why.

It's a family trait. Some call it 'Determination', others call it 'Yorkshire Grit', others like my Irish mother call it 'Sheer Bloody Mindedness', or 'Typical Bloody Yorkshiremen Too Tight To Buy Proper Tackle!'

But I know that using such ancient equipment reminded Uncle George of his dad, the old man with white eyes, which was probably the reason for him to use it.

Johnny Gray

My other Grandad was also a product of adversity and conflict, this time not in France or Belgium, but much closer to home, in Ireland.

Johnny Gray was an Irishman and like George Henry, Johnny was also a fisherman of some fame. He was known throughout County Monaghan, his home county, and even over the border in Counties Fermanagh and Tyrone the name of Johnny Gray was held in high regard among sportsmen.

Johnny lived in Clones in Co Monaghan, an historic little town but one which had the great misfortune in 1921 to straddle the border between the new Irish Free State, and British Northern Ireland. It was not an easy place to live in the 1920s.

First there was the murderous War of Independence when the IRA fought the British (who then ruled Ireland.) When the peace treaty between Britain and the so-called Irish Free State was signed on December 6th 1921 peace did not return, but on the contrary, a far more bloody and brutal Civil War broke out in the Free State, between pro and anti-Treaty Irishmen.

Even when that war was ended life around Clones was very dangerous for Protestants like Johnny Gray, because the new Catholic Free State viewed Protestants as being pro-British, and wanted rid of them. The IRA determined to drive them out of their new, and very Catholic, state. Over the next thirty years, the Protestant population declined by two thirds.

Johnny, who had no interest in politics or religion, somehow survived this mayhem, concentrating on raising a family, running his bicycle business and spending his spare time fishing or shooting. He was a very friendly and popular man in the town and in time he became a noted sportsman with both his fishing rod and his rifle. After the 1920s life in Clones settled down to one of relatively peaceful co-existence.

As kids over from England, my brother and I spent every summer with Johnny, at his house on the outskirts of Clones. Every day, rain or shine, we would go fishing with him.

His methods were astounding. "Boys, ye need a big bait to catch a big fish," he would say.

And when he said Big Bait, he meant a BIG bait. He had forearms like Popeye, probably as a result of hefting these giant lures across the local waters. If he was spinning in Lough Erne he would use heavy spoons nearly a foot in length, great red lumps of metal dripping with enormous treble hooks, that were a risk to the ears and lives of anyone within casting distance. These clattering monsters he would hurl a hundred yards and more across the waters. We used to joke that if he didn't hook the fish, at least he'd give them a headache.

Johnny had brightly-coloured pike plugs the size of guinea-pigs. He had big brown furry things that looked like rabbits loaded with meat hooks, but boy, could he catch fish. He kept his eyesight to the end, and though only possessing the one good leg, was a keen fisherman to his final days. His skill was so well-known that it was even mentioned in his obituary. This is from the local paper, *The Northern Standard*:

"The death has occurred at the age of 70 years in Monaghan County Hospital of Mr John Gray, Clones, who had been associated with the business life of the town for almost 60 years. His premises alongside the Farmyard, where he carried on a cycle sales and repair business, were a centre for conversation and exchange of views.

Generations of school children from rural districts called there to have their cycles repaired and Johnny was never known to disappoint any of them, with or without reward. Popular with everyone, he was a noted sportsman and a noted marksman with the small-bore rifle. There was a very large attendance of all creeds and classes at the funeral, which took place at Clones Presbyterian cemetery on Saturday."

'Popular with everyone… all classes and creeds…' that is the obituary of a real fisherman.

I remember the last day we ever saw him alive. It was at the New Bridges at Lisnaskea, and we were fishing a white-capped and windswept Lough Erne. My brother and I were by then cocky teenagers, and we were full of the latest methods from England. We had new tackle, we read *Angling Times* and *Trout and Salmon*, and to tell the truth, we felt rather embarrassed to see old Grandad and his crude methods.

Scorning to fish for pike, we were swing-tipping (then the latest method) for bream, and we were catching a sackful. Old Johnny by then could barely walk, and was lying there almost flat on his back, propped up against a pile of rocks.

"What're you after Grandad?" we teased as we watched him struggle to hurl out his giant spoon. He didn't have the energy to reply.

Bream after bream we hauled in. Bream are at best a pretty dull and uninspiring fish to catch, but at least they were fish. Johnny had caught nothing. We revelled in our teenage cleverness and slyly laughed at him.

We didn't know it, but Johnny was in great pain, for the old gammy leg had given out on him, and the creases in his face showed it. But he could still come fishing with us, still wanted to show us how to do it, even though we were young and thought we knew it all, with our new tackle and methods and our heads full of fishing articles.

BAM!

His old spinning rod went arcing over.

Someone saw it curve, and yelled, "He's got one! Your Grandad!"

Amused, we put down our bream rods and hurried over to watch Grandad struggling with his fish.

It was a pike. Not a monster by Lough Erne standards, but a good heavy double figure fish, that fought and splashed and took every ounce of old Johnny's failing energy to land it.

He was so exhausted by the end that he couldn't speak – or perhaps wouldn't speak, who knows? But the pride showed on his face, as we stood there with the net swinging with the weight of his magnificent gleaming green pike.

He died a couple of weeks later.

And I never even got time to tell him how much I thought of him.

Old Johnny Gray gave me the spirit of a real fisherman. Then my own Dad taught me the rudiments of catching fish. The rest I picked up myself, or from others, like James Blades, the legendary Hawes fisherman, who once invited this callow youth into his home and took him fishing on the River Ure. He taught me that to tie fishing flies is one thing, to be able to use them properly is quite another.

Early Days

I began fishing on the Nidd at Knaresborough, in what was then the West Riding of Yorkshire, with a bamboo rod bought for me in Ireland by my parents, for five shillings. I was about four years old. All I could catch were minnows. As Dame Juliana said of the minnow in her book, 'The Treatyse of Fysshynge with an Angle', the first fishing guidebook: 'though his body be little, yet he is a ravenous biter and an eager one' – and that was certainly true of the Nidd minnows.

I used to sit there on the grassy banks of the 'free stretch' opposite Conyngham Hall, with a bright red float and a hook with two foot of line and a worm on it, staring until my eyes stung at the leafy black water and leaping with excitement every time the float started to bob.

Ah, you couldn't buy that feeling for any amount of money. Four years old, and your float has just gone under…

If only we could step back in time.

I found early on in my fishing career that I didn't like maggots. For one thing they cost money, of which we didn't have a lot. For another, maggots had to come from a shop, which meant advance planning, which has always been a part of fishing I have avoided. Fishing has to be spontaneous and natural to me. A day comes when I say to myself, I'm going fishing. And I want to be able to get my tackle and go, just like that, not to have to go to shops and buy bait. It may sound trivial, but to me it's important.

Worms were free, and still are, though I believe there are some fishermen who actually spend money and buy worms. Incredible. Not done in Yorkshire! All I had to do to find my bait was dig in an uncultivated bit of our garden and find some nice juicy worms. And I could be on the riverbank in five minutes.

There I'd be, in Cherry Tree Deep, where my dad once found a drowned woman, and there I'd sit happily all day long, with my four inch snake of a worm threaded on my size 10 hook. I sometimes wondered why I never caught much, but it never really bothered me. After all, catching fish is only a small part of fishing, isn't it?

Mind you, my float used to bob up and down a lot.

"Bite!" I'd yell, and tug at the rod.

There was never anything on, unless I happened to foul-hook some poor unfortunate fish who just happened to be passing. The massive worm ensured that the only way I would land anything would be if the worm strangled something.

I fished like this for years, and it wasn't until I was eight or nine that I refined my technique, and began catching real fish.

A Gudgeon fisherman

Constant failure never depressed me. I was quite happy failing to catch the minnows which nibbled the ends off my python worms, but then I read *Mr Crabtree Goes Fishing*, and this changed my life.

I learned of fish called carp and roach and tench - subtle and intelligent fish which didn't fall for sucker baits like great fat lobworms. There were also immense and wonderful fish called barbel, who lived on the bottom of rivers, and which could only be caught by legering.

I threw away my big red float and bought a shilling's worth of coffin leads. I still used worms, for the aforementioned reasons. I had to hope that any Nidd barbel might suspend their critical faculties long enough to fall for a well-presented worm, instead of some more exotic fare like boiled potatoes.

I still had no idea what ground bait was, though I did throw in handfuls of soil every now and then, in the fond belief that this might do some good.

Alas no. Though I now knew that little fish lived at the surface and the big ones lived at the bottom, I was still no nearer landing any of the elusive denizens of the deep. I once found a dead chub and took that home, claiming I'd caught it, but no-one believed my stories of landing it after an epic duel. Everyone said it had been dead for weeks.

Then I caught my first gudgeon. Do not disparage gudgeon. Gudgeon are great little fish, which ounce for ounce can fight as well as any fish in the river. The only trouble with gudgeon is that they don't have many ounces to play around with. In fact the British Rod Caught Gudgeon Record is only around four ounces. Still, they are good little fighters, and to an eight year old reared on a diet of failure and minnows, gudgeon are a pretty big deal.

They're silvery bottom feeders with barbules on their chins. Actually they bear more than a passing resemblance to their giant cousins, the barbel, which led me into several unsuccessful attempts to pass off my catch of gudgeon as a netful of small barbel. No-one believed me, yet again.

I enjoyed catching them and I'd probably still have been there on the banks of the Nidd to this day, happily pulling out eight or nine gudgeon in an afternoon, getting sunburnt and a huge appetite. Gudgeon fishing did me no harm, and I look back with fond memories on the struggles I had with these little fish.

Unfortunately, the Big Wide World had to intrude and it came along and destroyed my childish innocence. The Big Wide World in this instance being a horrible snobbish boy called Peter Dyson, who lived near us (but definitely NOT in our road.)

Peter Dyson saw me one day as I was walking down to the river, carrying my ready-tackled-up rod. I had by this time broken the cane one, and was using a most unusual rod my dad had made for me from a tank aerial. (He was at Catterick Camp at this date, working for the Army.) It was as whippy as hell and didn't mind being stood on, made as it was out of some very tough and flexible steel, steel strong enough to resist being run over by a Soviet tank.

My dad had whipped the rings on with bright red silk he nicked from my mum's embroidery box. I thought the rod looked great, especially with a neon orange float already attached.

This Peter had no friends. He was not very intelligent, but went to some sort of special school for the sons of wealthy but stupid people. They wore chocolate brown school uniforms and yellow and brown striped caps and they didn't associate with us kids from the local school, who according to the Dysons were 'common.'

Peter Dyson spoke differently from the rest of us. To my untutored ear he sounded affected and pretentious with his lisping and sibilant hisses. We were quite happy speaking as everyone else did in our little town, but not the Dysons. They were posh.

Anyway, this particular day, there I was, happy as a lad can be when the sun is shining and it's the holidays and he's off fishing with Johnny Hopper and Teddy Sherman, his two best friends (even though they both live on a Council estate and are the sort of boys the Dysons would probably call delinquents.)

Then I saw this Peter leaning over the front gate of his detached house. I felt sorry for him being on his own, and thought of offering to take him out fishing with me. His parents didn't allow him out to play with ordinary children, in case he became contaminated with polio, which was all the rage at that time.

"Hello Peter," I said. "Do you want to come fishing?"

He laughed scornfully. "Fishing?"

I couldn't see what was so funny. "You don't need anything, you can share my rod with me."

I held up my pride and joy, my lovely tank aerial, for him to see. "Come on," I said. "Your Ma won't mind. Ask her and I'll wait for you."

I think for a moment that he wavered, because he glanced back towards the house to see if his mother was watching him. But then years of expensive private school education raised their head.

"What would I want to go fishing with you for?"

This was hurtful, but was rather pathetic, coming from someone as obviously lonely as he was, so I laughed it off.

"Come on. We'll look after you. You won't fall in and drown."

He ignored my offer, but pointed at my tank aerial and sneered. "What do you think you're going to catch with that monstrosity?"

This time I really was hurt, but I tried not to show it. I loved my tank aerial.

"Gudgeon," I replied, in all innocence.

He roared with mocking laughter. "Gudgeon? What on earth are Gudgeon?"

"Fish. There's lots of them," I said, feeling my faith ebbing away. I could feel tears of anger rising in my eyes. By now I had more than I could stand of his smirking face.

Dyson turned away. "I wouldn't dream of coming."

I hit him as hard as I could with the tank aerial. It knocked him back over the gate and flat on his bony bum in the garden. I told you it was strong.

"Serves you right," I said triumphantly.

I should have just gone fishing and forgotten all about nasty snobbish Dyson, but I couldn't. I no longer wanted to go fishing. He had spoiled it all for me.

From that day on I was finished with gudgeon fishing. I was ashamed of my tank aerial. I had to be a trout fisherman, or I wasn't going to be a fisherman at all.

Our Eck

I am not the only fisherman in our family.

There is also my brother, Richard, known to me as Our Kid or Our Eck and known to everyone else by various names, many of them uncomplimentary. Eck is three years younger than me and he just about qualifies as a real fisherman, though there have been many occasions when his fishing credentials have been in doubt. For our Eck is of a very different temperament than yours truly.

When he was first born he was brought before our Grandma, George Henry's wife, Beatrice.

My dad, proud as he could be over his new son, asked his mother that fateful question, "Well Ma, what do you think of him?"

This was an important judgement for the family as our Grandma was reputed to have the gift of second sight, an uncanny and apparently well-proven ability to look successfully into the future and to predict outcomes. The listeners were naturally anxious to hear the results of her prophecies for Eck.

Grandma peered into the cot, took a long look at my brother's scrunched-up prune face, his weird tuft of tousled black hair sticking up like a squirrel's tail, the unmistakeable look of aggression on his baby face, and pronounced, "You'll have trouble with that one!"

There was a shocked intake of breath from the assembled family. No-one had ever said such a dire pronouncement. After all, the baby was newly arrived and therefore totally innocent of any crime, and yet here was Grandma making a doom-laden prediction for his future.

Unfortunately she was to be proved correct. We did

have trouble with that one. Grandma definitely did have second sight.

Eck has been a great brother and companion to me from the start of his life. As soon as he learned to talk it became obvious that he had a strong sense of humour and a wicked sense of fun. However, these two characteristics often combined to get him into trouble, and that was where his problems really began, because our Eck did not like authority. Authority of any form. He was a born rebel.

His mum was the only one who could tame him, but she was careful never to push him too far in case he erupted. And even Ma sometimes had to resort to the use of a big wooden clothes brush to enforce obedience. Anyone else had no chance. Eck would do what he wanted, when he wanted and no-one was going to stop him.

His father, our dad, was such an easy-going kind-hearted soul he never stood a chance with his youngest son. He would always seek to avoid confrontation, but if trouble broke out, he would always back down, anything to keep the peace.

Thus began the fun-filled, but always rather troubled life of Richard Harry. Our Kid. Our Eck.

And now to some fishing…

That first trout

I caught my first trout at Easby Abbey on the River Swale in May 1958, when I was eight years old.

By then we were living at Richmond in the North Riding, because my dad had been posted as an electronics instructor to 8th Signals Regiment at Catterick Camp. My brother and I loved living up there because it was wild and windswept, far from civilisation. My mother hated it for much the same reasons. My dad secretly agreed with his sons, but kept quiet for diplomatic purposes. He always agreed encouragingly when my mother talked of one day returning to the balmy South and as soon as she was out of sight, would cheerfully forget all about her complaints.

Richmond is on the Swale, one of the greatest trout rivers in England, and one of the best places to go on the Swale was Easby Abbey. There the river flowed wide and shallow and there were runs full of hefty trout, trout that you could see on a sunny summer's day. Trout you dreamed of catching.

Unfortunately, dreaming of catching them was about all I did. My minnow and gudgeon-catching skills counted for nought with the wily Swale trout. They scorned my python lobworms, they laughed at my big red floats, they fled at the sound of my approaching half-pound lump of coffin lead.

I tried all my skills and never once did I get within nibbling distance of a trout. All I ever managed to do was launch the top section of my tank aerial rod into the deepest darkest pool, just below the road bridge, much to the amusement of a group of foulmouthed urchins who laughed at me and called out, "Why not chuck the rest in while you're at it?"

I ignored them and fished on with my stump of a rod.

As kids at Richmond C of E school, we did little else but fight, tell exaggerated stories of our own prowess, and invent crazes. There was Hulahooping, at which I was unbelievably incompetent and therefore not interested. There was Dutch Arrows, which I was good at and therefore enjoyed. These were lengths of sharpened garden cane, launched by twisting a piece of twine round the shaft and hurling it overarm. They were lethal, if inaccurate, weapons and every kid in Richmond wanted one.

We went nesting and climbing trees. We told lies about the birds' nests we had discovered and about the height of the trees we could climb. But most of all, better than all these, was our talk of trout tickling.

This was a legendary method of catching trout and one which fascinated every kid in the school, except Thomas Evans, who had asthma and bronchitis and a permanently runny nose and a mother who wouldn't allow him to do anything strenuous, poor lad.

Everyone could see the trout. All you had to do was go down to the river and you could see them lying there in shoals – at the High Bridge, below the Castle, at the Falls, at the railway bridge – the river was so shallow and clear the trout were always visible and tantalisingly close. I think it was this perpetual temptation that gave trout-tickling its particular allure.

Trout tickling went something like this: the expert trout tickler creeps up behind a trout which is happily dozing in the sun. He carefully reaches his fingers under the belly of the trout. Then he begins stroking his fingers along the trout, an action which apparently induces such rapture in the trout that he fails to notice the wily trout tickler is sliding his crafty fingers all the way up the trout's body, so that eventually he has his whole hand right round the fish.

Then the tickler gives a quick squeeze and flips the trout out onto the river bank. Brilliant. A work of genius.

And something every boy in Richmond dreamed of doing.

It beat Hula Hoops. It beat Dutch Arrows. It even beat being Robin Hood, the second favourite dream of Richmond's child population.

At this point we return to a warm and sunny day in 1958. I am eight years old. My brother Eck is five and wearing a heavy metal caliper encasing his leg, the result of his severing his Achilles tendon the previous year, when he fell through some panes of glass we had 'found' in the builders' shed next to our house. He can however still walk, as long as I give him a lift over the high stone walls.

With us is Norma Greensit, who is ten years old and who is a girl. No-one likes her, but we are afraid to tell her to go away, because she is a foot taller than any of us, and has bony fists and a violent temper. She obviously has not heard the rhyme about little girls being sugar and spice and all things nice. Norma Greensit is not nice. She tells filthy stories that give us all bad dreams and she tries to get us to show her our willies. Her nickname is Norma Greenshit.

Also present is Kenneth Greensit, younger brother of the dreadful Norma. Kenneth nettles himself, wets his pants, cuts his hands, falls from trees and is generally not safe to be let out on his own. A couple of months after this day Kenneth is run over by a car, and though run over by both sets of wheels, suffers no appreciable damage. I tell my dad that this is because the car has run over Kenneth's head.

Another member of our gang today is Clive Lawson. He is a Southerner from Abingdon so he has a posh accent which all us Yorkshire kids hate. He is known as the Pater's son, because he calls his dad a Pater, a ridiculous piece of affectation which gets him heartily abused every time he uses it.

Clive is a bit of a know-all and has an arrogant streak which gets him into constant fights. Despite this I sometimes like him because he is clever and inventive, so even though he can be very irritating at times, I still call him a friend and allow him to accompany us. Clive Lawson's mum makes homemade ginger beer and we know that if we take him out of her way for the day she will give us glasses of this delicious drink when we return. For no-one likes Clive Lawson much, not even his mother.

We set off from our house, and on the way we pass the Marcham's house. Alex Marcham is riding his blue racing bike on their drive. Alex, a boy of my own age, calls out. "Where you going?"

"Trout tickling."

"Can I come?"

"Course."

I wait for him to park the bike, and as I am waiting, who should appear but Alex's delectable sister, Sandra. My heart starts beating wildly at the sight of her pretty face.

She sees us, waves, and comes over to me. "Hello," she says with a big smile.

I am very much in love with Sandra, and find it hard to say anything beyond, "Hello."

Luckily for me, she is not so incapable of speech. "Can I come too?"

Can she come too? Are you kidding? I have dreamed of this moment for weeks, ever since we rolled over and over on their lawn and ended up looking into each other's eyes and nearly kissing.

I mumble something unintelligible, and she puts her hand on mine.

"I'll just get a jacket," she says, and I watch mesmerized

as she runs off to the house.

We walk the two or three miles down to Easby Abbey. Sandra walks beside me, and occasionally bangs into me or brushes against my leg. An electric shock thrills through my body at each touch.

At Easby there is an old ruin which we do not bother with, as it is just piles of rocks and costs 6d to get in. None of us has any money and we're all anxious to get to the river anyway. I want to be alone with Sandra. My brother and Clive and Alex want to tickle trout. Norma Greenshit wants to sunbathe topless and Kenneth Greensit, who can guess what he wants to do?

Here we are, the river at last. It is low and clear and wide. Boulders stick out. In some places it is possible to go out a long way on these boulders without getting wet. I do this at speed, hoping to impress the watching Sandra. Kenneth Greensit tries to copy me, slips and falls in. He howls and cries, sobbing pitifully until his sister slaps him and calls him a crybaby.

My brother is sitting on the grass, laughing at this, his bad leg stretched out in front of him. Clive Lawson, wading nearby, suddenly looks up and shouts, "Train!"

We all look up from the water to the woods on the far bank. Back towards town we can see the white puffs of smoke and steam from an engine leaving the railway station. Soon the noise reaches us, proving sound travels slowly. The engine makes a lot of noise, chuffing up enough energy to drag its coaches through the woods. The chuffs come slowly at first, then build up speed.

"There it is!" Alex shouts, and the engine emerges from the trees, black and powerful and thundering a tower of white clouds high into the blue summer sky. Birds scatter, cows stop chewing and watch.

The train clatters by, hissing and spitting steam at us. The black-capped driver leans out and waves and we all wave back, laughing and smiling. Six maroon coaches follow through. We stand in the river, watching it go round the curve and steam out of sight, though we can still hear the noise as it puffs its way down Swaledale towards Darlington and the big wide world.

As the day gets hotter, we take our wellies and socks off and stand barefoot in the river. We are trying to catch little fish called bullheads, which live under flat stones. We lift these stones carefully and peel them back, hoping each time that a dozing bullhead will be revealed. Sometimes there is nothing there. Sometimes there is a bullhead, which vanishes with a flick of its tail and a spurt of dirt. But sometimes the bullhead just sits on undisturbed.

Then we bend slowly over it and dunk our fingers slowly and carefully into the water, some way behind the fish. Showing no movement, we work our way into a position where we can get our fingers almost to touch the bullhead. When we're ready, we pounce.

Sometimes there's just a fleeting touch of the fish, before it's escaped. Sometimes we miss entirely. But sometimes we've got him, we cup him in both hands, leap and shout, "I've got one!" and carry him triumphantly to the stock pool where all our catch is being kept for the day.

Norma Greenshit keeps lifting her dress and allowing us to see what she fondly imagines is an enticing glimpse of her knickers. We all ignore her. Catching bullheads is much more exciting. Anyway, she has these baggy green ones on that just do nothing for me.

Kenneth Greensit has been poking a stick into a fresh green cowclap and has managed to smear some over himself.

Clive Lawson is bending over the fish pool. He shouts triumphantly, "Mine's bigger than yours! Mine's bigger than yours!"

Norma pricks up her ears at this and makes some comment, but Clive is talking about bullheads, not anything that might interest her.

I forget about him and turn away from her to check our Eck is safe and well. He sometimes forgets he is a cripple and tries to join in with us, just as if he had two good legs, and so I have to look after him.

This exaggerated sense of brotherly responsibility is a direct result of his severed Achilles tendon – which was largely my fault. He was only copying me in jumping over the glass panes, when he fell through one and sliced his Achilles in two. Alex Marcham had been with us, but had run away and abandoned us when our kid screamed. We haven't forgiven him for his cowardice.

"Alright our kid?"

He glances up, half asleep in the sun and grins. "Yeah," he says. "I'm just going to have a kip, then I'm going to throw stones at Alex Marcham."

Alex glares up from the water, where he is bent over, trying unsuccessfully to catch bullheads. "Just you try it," he threatens.

Our kid grins and taunts him. "You wouldn't hit a cripple would you?"

Alex Marcham flushes and bends his head once more to the water at his feet.

I'm now some distance away from them all, wading through water which is perhaps six inches deep. I've put my wellies back on, because I'm intending to go through the woods with Sandra to the Mill Race, to watch the huge trout which live there and to be alone with her in the darkness of the old mill.

Suddenly my foot slips. I've trodden on something slippery. I stumble, thinking 'what's happening?' My head goes down. I fall on one knee, face forwards into the water.

Clive Lawson sees me fall and laughs.

Our kid calls, "Are you alright bruv?"

Then I notice something in the water, under my foot. It's the head of a trout! I grab it, clasp both shaking hands round it and jerk it out of the water. I'm on my knees, holding it up, yelling, "I've got one! Look, I've caught a trout!"

The others all stop what they're doing and come running, while I hold it tighter and tighter to stop it escaping. It's a beauty, a red and black-spotted golden trout – and I've caught it! Tickled it. That's what I did. Yeah! I tickled it.

I struggle to my feet and wade ashore, where the others gather round to admire the fish.

"Bloody hell!" says Clive Lawson.

"What a beauty!" says our kid.

"It's only a fish," says Norma.

Clive Lawson is so surprised he can't hide his envy. I swell with the pride of capture.

"What is it?" asks Norma.

"A trout," says our kid. "Who invited you to come anyway, smelly knickers?"

She wants to fight, but is ignored. We've caught a trout. I've caught a trout.

"How'd you get it?" asks Clive Lawson.

I look him straight in the eye, my fish held between the two of us. "Tickled it of course," I say nonchalantly.

He'd obviously like to sneer and scoff, but how can he when the evidence is there in front of him?

I hand the fish over to my brother. "You look after this one our kid. I want to see if I can tickle one for you as well."

Clive is so utterly defeated he mooches off on his own, morosely throwing stones at the far bank.

I wink at my brother.

He asks quietly, "Did you really tickle it?"

"Sort of. I tickled it with my boot."

Further conversation is suspended because Kenneth has decided he wants to tickle trout too, and has picked up a large heavy boulder, which he can barely support. He is now staggering about with the boulder above his head, a danger to himself and to anyone within reach of the boulder. For once I am prepared to help him save himself, because today, today, I have become a tickler of trout. I catch him and lift the boulder from above his head, placing it safely on the grass.

"You should have left him," says Norma in disgust. "Stupid little twat might have killed himself."

I ignore her, for today she cannot annoy me, today I am a tickler of trout! I can't wait for Monday. The news will be all round school.

Clive Lawson won't give up easily, I'll give him that. On the way back home, he asks again, "Are you sure you tickled it?" He speaks with more than a hint of suspicion.

"Course I did. How else do you think I caught it?"

The others all laugh, and Clive Lawson blushes.

I bear the trout home, flushed with the pride of being the first kid at Richmond school to actually tickle a trout in front of witnesses.

The following Monday at school I am a hero. Kids keep coming up to me and asking in awed terms how I did it. I am a star. For the first time in my life I have gangs of admirers. Kids fight with each other for the honour of being in my gang. I have reached such a dizzy height of power that I no longer have to do my own fighting, which is a constant part of life at our school. Several of the would-be trout ticklers make excellent surrogate brawlers.

Clive Lawson is absolutely green with envy, mooching around the playground muttering to himself. He is the one and only dissenter. Everyone else is convinced I am possessed of the power. I am a trout tickler extraordinaire!

Kids ask, "Can I come with you next time you're going?"

I modestly agree, with the proviso that I might not be going for a week or two, as I am going to Knaresborough with my dad (a crafty escape clause I dreamed up overnight.)

Then word reaches me via gleeful girl disciples (who want to see a fight) that Clive Lawson has been telling stories about me. He has been heard muttering words of untruth. He does not believe I tickled the trout. On the contrary, he has been heard to say that I am a fraud, that I am making fools of them all, and that my capture of the trout was a total fluke.

My followers are outraged.

"Gob him!"

"Smack his head in!"

"Everybody hates him!"

And from the girls, "He's just jealous cos you got one and he didn't! So sort him out!"

I should have been content with what I'd got. I had power and status for the first time in my life. Perhaps it was this that went to my head and led me to confront him. Instead of ignoring Clive, who was totally isolated anyway, I foolishly had to go up to him and challenge him, didn't I?

"What's this you're saying about me Clive?"

"You didn't tickle that trout!"

"Course I did."

"No you didn't!"

"How come I caught it then?"

The gathered crowd turned accusingly to Clive, who defiantly stood his ground.

"Because you trod on it."

There was a gasp from the crowd. They turned to me. I tried to laugh at the absurdity of such a suggestion, wishing I'd kept quiet and not started this discussion, but it was too late.

"Well, did you?" a girl called aggressively.

"Don't be ridiculous!" I tried.

"Alright then," Clive countered. "If you tickled it, how come it had a bloody great welly print on its back?"

The crowd gasped again. I should have laughed it off, but I was too slow. I blushed with the truth of what he had said.

The watchers saw it instantly, and I was finished.

"Ha!" Clive crowed. "Told ya!"

My defenders and admirers vanished in a second. Within minutes the news was all round school. I wasn't a trout tickler after all. I was a fraud. I had trodden on it. It was a fluke. I was just an ordinary mortal, like the rest of them.

My moment of power had gone.

I learned my lesson. It was a painful one at the time. It taught me not to gloat over anyone, even someone I despised.

I lived it down eventually. I forgot the humiliation and the mocking remarks. I even forgot Clive Lawson, who moved away down South to live where he belonged. But somehow I never forgot that first trout. The one I tickled to death.

A Swale failure

My fishing skills developed slowly over the years. As the worms I used gradually became smaller, so the fish I caught gradually became larger. I developed into a contender for the British Rod-Caught Bullhead Record. I began to dream of collecting my Sunday Express Prize Rod. I stopped hurling rocks into the river when I had failed to catch anything. In short, I became a fisherman.

There were hiccups along the way. I lost the beautiful black Mitchell reel my mum and dad bought for Santa to give me. I had attached it firmly to my rod (or so I thought) but one day when I was inching my way across the pipe bridge over the swirling Swale, it fell off, and landed, as these things have a way of doing, not on some soft grassy bank from where it might easily be retrieved, but straight into a black whirlpool, from where there was certainly going to be no recovery.

I kept the loss secret from my parents for months, until one holiday Saturday my dad asked if he could come fishing with me, and then the secret was out. There was no disguising the fact that my nylon line was tied direct to the end of my rod, and that I was retrieving line by hand. I couldn't merely pretend that this was some arcane method of fishing.

Strangely enough, my dad didn't berate me for this loss. I think he realised how much I felt it already.

The reel wasn't replaced though. Santa was broke.

I saved up and bought one of the first items of Japanese fishing tackle to come onto the market, a fishing rod. It was FIVE pieces of bamboo in a bag, all for the affordable price of £2.7s 6d and it seemed to me to be an amazing amount of tackle for the price.

It consisted of a short two-piece spinning rod and what appeared to be a three-piece leger or perhaps float rod. I was quite entranced by my new acquisition, despite the disparaging comments made by everyone who saw it.

"Japanese?" they scoffed. "Don't tell me the Japanese make fishing tackle!"

('Japanese' in the 1950s being a by-word for something cheap, nasty and easily-broken – a far cry from the stylish and efficient gear they produce nowadays.)

When I assured them that they did indeed make fishing tackle, then the reaction changed to a cynical inspection of my wonderful new rods.

"Bright, aren't they?" was the consensus. "Going to dazzle the trout into submission?"

I ignored such wounding remarks. I knew my so-called friends were only jealous. I liked the rod's shiny chrome and gaudy green silk fittings.

The criticism and the mockery remained however. Somehow people could never come to terms with the fact that the Japanese had dared to make fishing tackle. Nasty cheap transistor radios yes, but fishing tackle? Surely not. Only the British made fishing tackle.

When I proudly showed them the MADE IN JAPAN label just above the butt, the reaction was universal.

"What a load of rubbish!"

Rubbish maybe, but where are the Japanese now? And more to the point, where are all the British manufacturers gone, who used to outclass them so clearly?

It wasn't very good tackle. The spinning rod was too short and stiff and you couldn't spin on the Swale anyway, it was too shallow and rocky. I tried it once, and hurled a

Devon Minnow across the big pool just below the bridge next to the railway station, which was a big mistake for two reasons.

One, the far shore was a vertical rocky cliff reaching to the river's edge.

Two, all the passers-by on the bridge could see me as I cast out. The Devon Minnow, my one and only expensive lure, landed in a crevice on the far rocky cliff, where it was impossible to reach. The onlookers roared with laughter as I leaped up and down in frustrated rage.

For all I know that Devon Minnow is there to this day. As a result of this debacle I abandoned spinning and have rarely touched it since.

The leger/float rod did neither very well. It was too soggy for a leger rod, having a six-inch droop, even without the hefty coffin lead at the far end. When loaded and ready for casting it was so soft and floppy it used to drag along the ground. Each time I flicked it back to cast I winced, feeling certain the rod would snap.

The rod used to whip the old lead out, I'd give it that. I regularly peppered the far bank with coffin leads. I'll bet that they're still there, along with my beautiful and much-missed Devon Minnow. I expect I caused lead poisoning among a fair percentage of the riverbank's inhabitants.

Nor was the rod any more effective when used for float fishing. The flopping sag in the middle of the rod did little to assist my striking when float fishing. Mind you, I was still using my beloved big red Irish perch bungs – colourful things, but not exactly responsive to the subtle bites of a roach or a trout. I used to sit there waiting for the fish to tug that brute of a float under the water. A fifteen-pound pike would have had a job.

Still, I persisted.

I used all the wrong tackle. I used all the wrong methods and I caught very few fish.

Ireland

How different it was when we went to Ireland. There even I could catch fish.

Every summer we went to stay with Grandad Johnny at his house in Clones, Co Monaghan. Clones is an ancient town, known for its mediaeval Round Tower, its turbulent history, and above all, for its fabulous fishing, for Clones is absolutely surrounded by rivers and lakes (known as loughs in Ireland.)

Grandad had a bicycle shop at the bottom of Fermanagh Street, the main street of Clones. It was a busy little town and Grandad's shop was ideally placed, being next to the railway station, the Creighton Hotel and the main road to Newtownbutler, the nearest town.

Grandad Johnny was a very well-known figure in Clones. His bicycle shop not only sold bicycles, but repaired them, and at a time when few people owned cars but nearly everyone had a bicycle, it was a prosperous and thriving business. Johnny's shop was a place where everyone brought their bikes for Johnny and his team of assistants to repair the punctures and breakages.

Johnny was a popular character in the town. An amusing and gregarious man, he allowed any callers to his shop the time to sit and have 'a wee word' as he called it. The wee word might last the whole morning, for Johnny cared little about time. As a result the shop was always packed, as anyone who called would be made welcome. People would sit around the sales area and the workshop, so that Johnny Gray's place became a focal point of the little town.

Johnny himself was an excellent sportsman, despite a leg injury from his youth. He was a renowned shot and an expert fisherman. With his great friend Paddy The Worm

Man, there was not a lough or river around Clones that Johnny hadn't fished.

And every July we would arrive to join the fun.

Grandad took us to loughs so clear and fertile you could see great ferny forests beneath the boat, with shoals of fish swimming about. We caught boatfuls of lovely gold and red rudd, on lumps of bread paste, called 'dough' by Grandad. The Irish rudd didn't seem to mind that we were using our big red perch bungs, unlike those snooty Swale trout.

And then there were the pike. Even now I retain some of my childhood feelings for pike – a mixture of fear and respect for these immense predators of the deep. In some of the Irish loughs, on a day when they were feeding, they would attack anything. They'd rocket after our spinners, lunging at them like great green torpedoes, right alongside the boat. They'd launch themselves at any bait. They could see us, they knew what we were and what we were after, but they weren't scared. They were hungry and in the mood for killing.

One day my dad caught a pike when he wasn't even fishing. We were all out on a lough in an old boat: Grandad, his pal Paddy the Worm Man, my dad, Eck and me. Our dad was just sitting there in the back of the boat, daydreaming away as usual, with his spinner lying still at the end of his rod, which he'd parked against the side of the boat. The spinner wasn't even in the water, but dangling in the air, about six inches above the surface of the lough.

Suddenly there was a splash and a flash of green and a great snout full of teeth. A pike had leapt out and grabbed the spinner. Everyone yelled PIKE!! And my dad nearly fell out of the boat in his haste to seize the rod before it disappeared into the lough.

Luckily the pike was so ferocious it had swallowed the spinner, two sets of trebles and about a foot of steel trace. Even my dad, who had been half asleep at the time, could manage to land it safely. I don't know who was more surprised - my dad or the pike.

English people who have never been to Ireland tend to scoff at these stories, thinking they are untrue, or exaggerated. I can honestly say that every fishy tale I tell about Ireland is completely true, for as old Johnny used to say, "In that lough thur's pike so big you could put a saddle on thum!"

My brother and I spent every summer in Ireland, packed off at the beginning of each holiday from the little station at Richmond. We went all the way by train – something that couldn't be done nowadays. And we did it by ourselves – another thing that probably wouldn't be possible today for a couple of young boys on their own.

Then, in the first week of September, we would return to Richmond after tears and protestations that we didn't want to leave Ireland. But as soon as we were home and back with our mum and dad and Frisky the cat and all our pals, and as soon as we had told them all our adventures and had them all dismissed as fantasy, the reality of life as a fisherman in the Yorkshire Dales returned.

There were no fabulous fish on the Swale, only trout, trout which I so conspicuously failed to catch. It didn't matter how many times I told my friends that I'd caught lots of fish in Ireland, where the fish were so much bigger and fiercer than these Swale tiddlers, it didn't make any difference.

They still said, "Those Irish fish must be stupid."

"Why?" I'd ask.

"'Cos they let YOU catch 'em!"

I was still a failure. No matter what stories of Irish success I might relate, I was still not a real fisherman, in my own eyes or anyone else's. Because, as yet, I hadn't caught one single Swale trout. Apart, that is, from the one I tickled to death.

The Gold-Ribbed Hare's Ear

My first real rod-caught trout came about through two big changes in my fishing technique. Firstly, I discovered the existence of some marvellous little things called trout flies, and secondly, I discovered that the Japanese leger/float rod I had been struggling so unsuccessfully with for the past year, was in fact a fly rod.

One of my Dad's army friends at Catterick Camp gave him an old Hardy's catalogue of their fishing flies. If you haven't seen one of these you've missed something amazing. Even now as I sit and look at it I can hardly believe this is the work of a commercial company and not a work of art. There are pages and pages of beautiful colour reproductions of every type of fishing fly – far superior to anything I've ever seen in modern fishing books. And this was just a fishing catalogue, a list of their goods for sale.

On finding the book, I seized it and pored over it for months. To this day I can remember the excitement of discovering for the first time, those wonderful words - Gold-Ribbed Hare's Ear. A fly called a Gold-Ribbed Hare's Ear. Not just an ordinary common or garden Hare's Ear, but a Gold-Ribbed one. I sat and drooled at the pictures of such exotica.

My mum used to attack me with the metal Hoover tube, when she saw me reading the Hardy's book hour after hour.

"Get up off your backside and get some fresh air!" she'd shout. "Go on. Outside! It's not healthy sitting there staring at those oul flies."

I was so entranced I would have to be physically parted from the book before I would move. And that old Hoover tube could hurt the way she wielded it.

In winter I was usually excused going outside for the famous fresh air. No-one in their right mind goes out willingly to play in a Swaledale winter, not unless it's snowing and you can go sledging with your mates.

So, thanks to the marvellous Hardy's catalogue, I learned about trout flies. After my voracious and obsessive reading I soon knew all their names. I could talk knowledgeably about every variety of wet and dry fly, even though I'd never used one. And the names reflected their origins: from Wales came the wonderful Coch-y-bonddhu; from Scotland the Black Pennell and the Bloody Butcher (so menacing those two!) Ireland produced the Murrough and the Connemara and Black. From good old Yorkshire came North country patterns, the Waterhen Bloa, Snipe and Purple and Partridge and Orange. Rich English chalk streams produced Lunn's Particular. My hero, the legendary fishing writer GEM Skues, developed the Tup's Indispensable, the Blue Winged Olive, the Red Spinner and Red Sedge. Then there was GS Marryat, who had invented the eyed hook and the Pale Watery Dunn. Was there ever such poetry?

Unfortunately I didn't possess any of these wonderful flies, but that was a minor consideration. I could still drool.

I was also totally lacking in the knowledge of how to use them. I had no idea how to cast the fly out to the fish, which was, I realized, a bit of a handicap to my fishing success.

In those days there were no explanatory films or videos or YouTube advice on how to cast properly. The angling books I took out from the library talked airily about fly fishing lines, but they gave no explanation of what they were or how they were to be used.

Nor did it seem logical to me that a trout should want to go and eat a bit of feather. I could see that a big juicy worm would appeal to a hungry trout, but a bit of feather? And didn't they notice the hook sticking out of it? They hadn't been noticeably short-sighted about spotting the hooks embedded in my lobworms, so why should they ignore the much more obvious hook in a fly – even one so exalted as a Gold-Ribbed Hare's Ear. Were their critical faculties impaired by feathers and silk?

I had no-one to teach me. My English flyfishing Grandad was blind. Grandad Johnny in Ireland didn't go fly fishing. My dad knew all about resisters and oscillators, but nothing about such wonders as a Blue Winged Olive.

By now all the other kids I knew had abandoned fishing as just a passing phase, and were very much into courting. The boys spent their days chasing the girls around the fields trying to get them down on the ground for a snog. A sophisticated lot, the Richmond kids.

I wasn't bothered with this, unless the girl concerned was a certain Georgiana Hunte, a sylph-like creature in diaphanous skirts, brought to school and collected each day by her father in a big Jaguar car. She was about as likely to let herself be dragged down for a snog in some cowclap-ridden meadow as I was to catch a Swale trout, so I stuck to fishing.

If my pals weren't desperately trying to fondle girls in fields, they were talking passionately about someone called Elvis Presley, another of life's excitements which had somehow passed me by. No, as my friends had given up on fishing, I was on my own.

The library in Richmond, surprisingly, had nothing to help me advance my fishing skills. Libraries in those days in the late Fifties were very serious places, full of dark-spined books, not books for leisure activities like fishing.

Library assistants did not seem well-disposed to small

boys clutching five sections of Japanese fishing tackle who kept asking for books on fly fishing. Old men who reeked of tobacco kept telling me to shush or bugger off, so I gave up on the library as a source of information.

I was very shy, which didn't help me make progress. I sometimes saw anglers fly fishing on the river, but I was far too nervous to go up to a complete stranger and ask him how to fly fish, it just wasn't in me.

My fishing career stagnated. I knew that I wasn't going to make any progress unless I could find someone who could teach me how to cast flies.

Eventually, despairing of ever becoming a fly fisherman, I saved up some of my sixpences and went into Metcalfe's fishing tackle shop in the Market Place, and bought a fly to console myself. A Gold-Ribbed Hare's Ear, naturally.

I didn't go fishing with it. No chance, a Gold-Ribbed Hare's Ear? I kept it on my bedside table, and I used to lie there looking at it in wonder, entranced by its delicacy, its golden hackle, and above all, by the Gold-Ribbed wrapping around the body. It was my pride and joy for months.

Then my mum decided our bedroom was 'a festering pit' as she put it, and armed with a vacuum cleaner she launched into a massive clear-up operation one day when we were out at school. During this operation she sucked up my lovely fly in a fit of vacuuming zeal and my beautiful Gold-Ribbed Hare's Ear was no more.

Poor Ma. She couldn't understand what a heinous crime she had committed. No matter that I tearfully tried to explain to her that she'd sucked up my cherished and wonderful Gold-Ribbed Hare's Ear, she just clucked and said, "Nasty filthy things flies."

There was no getting round the fact that when it came to Fishing Soul, my mother had none.

Birth of a fly-tyer

I determined that I would tie my own flies. I stole silks from my mother's sewing basket, little round wooden bobbins with 'Dewhirst's Sylko' labels on each end.

I found a dead starling and plucked some feathers from its breast and wings. I put a size 8 hook in the vice in my dad's garage and tied the feathers round it. The resulting fly was kind of black and sooty and didn't look quite right somehow, compared to my memory of the beloved Gold-Ribbed Hare's Ear.

I showed my handiwork to my brother. "What do you think our kid?"

He recoiled in disgust. "It stinks!"

I moved it away from his face. "Yeah, but apart from that?"

"It looks like a bog brush."

I had to agree with him. There was more to tying flies than I had imagined.

I tried again. This time I made sure the feathers had no rotting flesh attached to them. I got the feathers from a dead crow I found on the road. This second attempt was an improvement and on contemplating the result I decided that I was quite chuffed with myself.

This gave me the opportunity to boast to my school friends that I had started tying my own trout flies.

"Oh yeah?" they sneered. "Like all them Irish fish you're supposed to catch!"

Having been challenged, I had to bring my fly into school to prove my fly-tying talents. I tucked the Crow fly carefully into a matchbox and pocketed it. Then, at school break, came the big moment.

"Where is it then? This fly you're supposed to have tied?"

It was with some considerable satisfaction that I opened the palm of my hand to reveal my Crow fly.

The response was uproar.

"Fly?" they howled. "More like a dead croggie!" (Croggie was Richmond language for a crow.)

A laughing mocking crowd gathered. "Come and look at Cluffie's croggie!"

And they all agreed. "What a bloody idiot!"

I was doing some suffering on behalf of my beloved angling, I can tell you.

I returned home humiliated, but determined to do better. My next fly would be smaller, neater and not based on a dead crow. I repaired to the garage, looking for the cat.

Then my mother started sniffing suspiciously around me. "What's that dreadful smell?"

I denied all responsibility, but she wasn't satisfied, going off to search the garage. Then she found the dead birds.

Fly tying was suspended until further notice.

Getting nearer

What I couldn't understand (because no-one had told me) was how you managed to cast the fly out into the river. I didn't know that you needed a special heavy fly line in order to cast the delicate and weightless fly.

I was used to chucking several ounces of coffin lead out to gain distance. Granted, the lead usually gave me too much distance – hence the lead-spattered far bank - but problems like that I could understand. What I could not see was how to send a fly, which weighed practically nothing, ten or fifteen yards out to where the fish were inevitably lying, under the opposite bank of the river.

My next step forward was to learn how to cast. This I tried in the road outside our house with my Starling fly and my Crow fly and my Japanese leger/float rod. A crowd led by Norma Greenshit and Clive Lawson gathered to watch, and, they hoped, to laugh. I didn't disappoint them.

I attached the Starling fly to the end of my usual fishing line – about twenty yards of oft-broken and many times re-knotted and twisted 8lbs B.S. nylon monofilament.

"Go on then Cluffy! Let's see what you can catch in our road!"

I ignored them.

A newcomer joined the happy throng. "What's he doing with a fishing rod in the middle of our road?"

I tried to cast, as I had seen fly fishers cast.

It just swished about hopelessly. No matter how hard I hurled the Japanese leger/float rod, it just would not cast out the fly. The watchers roared in delight.

"Caught owt yet?" Alex Marcham called, adding, to much ribaldry, "What do you usually catch on this bit of road?"

I ignored him and tried again. And failed again.

"Serves you right!" Norma taunted, from some unspecified hatred of her own.

I lost my temper. In a red-eyed rage, I lashed the air furiously, accidentally whipping poor gormless Kenneth Greensit across his bare legs with my Starling fly. He screamed and bled, running to tell his mother that I had whipped him. Fly fishing experiments in our road were suspended until further notice.

Would I ever learn how to fly fish properly?

The Kingfisher

Then, totally unexpectedly like all the best surprises, came the marvellous day when I discovered the secret. We were at Easby Abbey, my mum and dad having a picnic, my little brother being unusually restrained and obedient because of the caliper on his leg and his mum keeping her beady eye on him. I wandered off on my own, and soon came upon a man fly fishing.

He was standing in the river, wearing big black boots. He was swishing his rod, much as I had done in our road, but with considerably more success. He didn't crack any line, or hit the ground with his back cast. Instead, he lay his line in beautiful long curves across the water, putting the fly down delicately exactly where he wanted it to go. Such precision was a work of considerable skill, an art, and was simply wonderful to watch, every bit as aesthetically pleasing to me as a great painting.

Just as I was watching him, he rose a fish, struck quickly, and hooked it. I jumped up and ran to watch in excitement. What would I give to be able to do that? My left arm, at the very least.

He played the trout expertly, drawing it into the bank almost at my feet and wading ashore after it. He must have noticed how big my eyes were, because he brought the fish over to me.

"Now then young un," he said. "What do you think of that? A beauty, isn't it?"

I couldn't speak. Not only had this God landed one of the sacred Swale trout that I so lusted after, he had done so with a fly rod. I stared open-mouthed, first at the superb fish, and then at the tackle.

"Are you a fisherman?" he asked.

I managed to nod.

"I'd let you have a go with my rod," he said.

My heart leaped.

"But you'd need waders."

My heart nearly burst.

He glanced above his head, where the alder trees arched over the water. "Hmm. I'd let you have a go here, but it's too dangerous. You'd get snagged on the trees."

And then he did the most wonderful thing, he dragged the line in and held it up in his hands to show me what he was using.

"Greenwell's Glory," he said, showing me the fly.

I recognised it instantly from my Hardy's catalogue.

"They reckon that Black Spiders are better here, but the Greenwell is my favourite."

I understood exactly what he meant. It was his Gold-Ribbed Hare's Ear.

"And this is my line," he added. "It's a Kingfisher."

He drew the nylon line through his fingers from the fly upwards, until he came to a great thick piece of what looked like wire, leading back up the rod to the reel.

A Kingfisher? I couldn't believe how thick and crude it looked.

"But surely the fish see it?" I gasped aloud.

He laughed. "You've found your voice have you? Well, the answer is, yes, the fish can see it. If you give them the chance. The secret is to not give them the opportunity. You cast well above them, that way the fly drifts down to them as naturally as possible."

My mind was reeling. The secret was out.

TO CAST A FLY YOU HAD TO HAVE A SPECIAL FLY LINE.

No wonder I had been such a dismal failure! I said no more. I had seen enough. I now needed a Kingfisher line, as soon as humanly possible. I would sacrifice sweets, birthday presents, Christmas presents, everything, in order to possess one of those lines.

For with it, I was certain, I would one day catch a Swale trout on the fly.

Johnny's gift

I told my dad. I saved up. I wrote to Grandad Johnny. I did everything I could, but even so it was another six months before I got my fly line.

We were in Ireland and it was almost time to return to England. All summer there had been hints of a surprise, overheard talk of a secret present. I wished and prayed that it was the Kingfisher line of my dreams. I knew Grandad Johnny always gave us something to take back home with us. I had dropped enough hints; I kept dragging them all to look in the tackle shop window on Fermanagh Street, just to point out to them the Kingfisher line that was so alluringly on display there.

I had dropped so many subtle hints even my dad must have guessed what I was after. He kept saying, "We'll get you one of those maggot boxes you've always wanted," which was his way of saying he'd got the hint about the fly line.

A Kingfisher was expensive, I realised that, but I was willing to go without birthday and Christmas presents in order to get one, so surely they could stretch their finances just this once?

Departure day came. Grandad Johnny was silent and (I suspected) tearful that we were going. He said that this would be the last time we ever saw him alive and that he would probably die before our next visit, but I ignored this as he always said he was going to die before our next visit, and he never had done so far. And anyway, where was my fly line?

I was obsessed, selfish, totally fixated, I admit it. I wanted to see what leaving presents we were going to get.

My brother didn't want to go home and was being rebellious. "I hate home," he said. He hated mum and he hated Dad and he hated Yorkshire and he wanted to stay in Clones with Grandad for ever.

Grandad started crying.

Never mind all the tearful goodbyes, what I wanted to know was where the hell were the going-away presents?

In a moment of peace, I took advantage and threatened my brother that if he didn't shut up I'd thump him. He told Grandad, who said that I could go back to England, but he was keeping my brother. It looked like I would never get my Kingfisher line.

Then without warning, Grandad opened a drawer and took something out. "Here," said Grandad, handing me a packet. "It's for you. Take it."

I took it without second bidding and belted off into the other room, the Palace where no-one ever went because my grandma had died there. I ripped open the packet and could see immediately that it was a fly line.

"Yahoo!" I shouted. "Good old Grandad!"

Then a sudden horror hit me. The line was bright green and unnaturally shiny. A Kingfisher was dull brown and definitely not shiny. This line was plastic. A Kingfisher was made of waxed silk. This clearly wasn't the Kingfisher I had lusted after, but some cheap imitation.

'Stupid old Grandad!' I thought unkindly. 'He can't even get it right, not even when I showed him which one I wanted.'

It was in fact a nasty bright green plastic thing, tightly curled in its plastic see-through container. It was, of course, made in Japan, which in those far-off Fifties days meant it was a cheap rubbishy imitation of the wonderful British original. The Kingfisher of my dreams.

I went back to the leave-taking. "Thank you very much Grandad," I said, politely telling lies.

My brother was dragged off kicking and screaming and protesting he wanted to live in Ireland for ever. Grandad burst into tears and assured us once again that he would have died before we returned the following summer, and we left for England.

A fly fisherman

Getting the wrong fly line taught me one of the lessons of life I suppose – that every time something really good happens, there's always a little bit of bad thrown in as well, just so you keep things in perspective.

I was at last the proud possessor of a real fly line – the fact that it wasn't the one I wanted would just teach me not to be greedy and to expect presents. With the nasty green plastic thing I would just have to make the best of a bad job, and fish with it regardless.

I never ever managed to get the tight curls out of that Japanese fly line. I think it must have been one of the early prototype designs, made out of experimental pvc. However, I could at least cast a fly with it. Mind you, the line lay glistening on the water looking like coils of barbed wire. It must have startled every fish in the Swale between Marske and Topcliffe, but at least, I consoled myself, at least it's a fly line. And the old rod, freed for once from its half pound of coffin lead, could actually cast it out quite presentably.

I learned to cast in O'Brien's the builders' field, having been banished there by Kenneth's mum, Mrs Greensit, who feared, she said, for her son's eyesight when I was around. The woman was a fool, and I told my father so. He agreed, and suggested I go deep into the field at the back of our house, well out of sight of both Mother Greensit and Idiot Son Greensit.

This I did, and soon learned how to cast a fly line. It's not too difficult; it can be learned in a few hours. It's not like actually catching fish, which is difficult and cannot really be learned in an entire lifetime.

I deduced from what the fly fisherman had told me, that you tied a length of nylon called a leader between the fly and the fly line. This leader was very important, as it prevented the trout from seeing the actual fly line. I didn't know the knots, but improvised some of my own which after several tries, proved successful. I was, I realised proudly, well on the way to becoming a fly fisherman.

The waders were a luxury I would have to do without. I was used to standing in the Swale in my bare legs for hours on end anyway. Only softies needed waders. The net, the spare flies, they were all luxuries too. They could be bought in time, but all I needed for now was a proper shop-bought fly and I'd be a real fisherman at last.

I rifled my brother's piggy bank, beat him up when he discovered the theft and set off once more for Metcalfe's tackle shop – this time to buy a fly I was actually intending to use on fish.

It was a Greenwell's Glory. I was prepared to sacrifice my love of the poetic Gold-Ribbed Hare's Ear for the much more prosaic, but obviously effective, Greenwell. I had learned from experience that there are times when you have to leave beautiful dreams behind and adopt ordinary reality if you want to succeed – and that doesn't just apply to fishing.

I set off for the exact same spot where I had seen the man catch the fish, determined to copy his methods precisely, for the scent of Swale trout was upon me at last.

I'd like to be able to record that I was instantly successful, but I can't. I'd like to be able to tell lies and say that I persevered despite early failures and eventually came to catch trout on the fly, but I can't.

I failed all right, that was easy enough. Wading thigh-high without waders in April is a vastly different proposition from standing ankle-deep without waders in July. My legs froze. My testicles retracted deep inside my body. I stumbled and fell in. I soaked myself. I used words I had learned from the Lord Lovat's kids – a fearsome tribe of snot-caked loonies who lived in a rundown estate near our house. I tried everything I knew.

But I just couldn't catch fish.

With more experience I learned that the water was too high and coloured, or too cold for a fly hatch. That I would have been better off with one of my discarded lobworms, even some from the bag I had left forgotten in the garage, the worms that were to cause my mother such nausea later that month before they were discovered.

After each unsuccessful trip I returned home cold, wet and disconsolate, my dreams of a bagful of trout suddenly bitterly ironic.

Success at last

It was September and there were only a couple of weeks of the trout season left. The bad weather would soon set in and then I'd be confined to barracks and I'd never get a chance to go trout fishing again until next year. Next year! The prospect was so depressing.

I mooched around the house staring morosely at the streaming windows. Did other would-be anglers have to go through torments like this, I wondered. I doubted it. In my depression I felt that it was I alone who suffered.

My luck turned suddenly and without warning. The hot sun returned. An Indian Summer was officially proclaimed. The evenings stayed long and light. There were Teddy Boy riots in London. Each day I ran home from school, gathered up my tackle, and ran down to the river. Norma Greenshit said that if I continued to ignore her advances she would never forgive me, and would turn to other men.

I ignored her, gratefully.

And then it happened. I caught my first trout. It may have been an accident. The fish may well have hooked itself while I was looking the other way. It may have been a case of suicide by a trout tired of life. But I didn't care. I hooked him just the same.

I can't honestly say that I played it in the textbook manner – my style was more of a frantic yerk towards the bank than the more sophisticated techniques of a chalk-stream fisher. Halford would have winced. GEM Skues would not have been impressed.

I swung it into the shallows, yelling in my excitement. Then I pounced on it, hugging it to my chest in delight, hardly able to believe that my dreams had come true at last.

I practically kissed it, so overjoyed was I.

As I lifted it out of the water the hook fell out and I had to squeeze the trout tight to prevent its escape. There it was, lying on the grass in front of me. I knelt in worship in front of it. A beautiful silvery fish, with a golden chest and flanks covered in freckles of red and dark grey. I just sat and stared and smiled.

I suppose I should have killed it. I should have taken it home and shown it off as evidence of my new-found skill. It would have saved a lot of difficulty in the near-future, but I couldn't do it. I couldn't kill that first fish, not after all it had done for me.

I wet my hands, cupped the fish gently in both palms, and lowered it back into the fast-running water. It flicked its tail and was gone, and with it all the evidence of my fishing prowess. I stood up, an older and wiser man. I had done it. I was a fisherman at last.

I told them all about it at home. "I caught one!" I panted, breathless after running all the way back from the river.

"Trout for tea eh! Good lad!" said my dad.

My mum, dad and brother all crowded round me as I unpacked.

"Well?"

"Well what?"

"Let's have a look at it then."

I paused. "Oh."

They glanced at each other.

"What are you looking like that for? I put it back."

"Okay son, course you did," said dad, and to my mum, he said, "Better get some fish fingers on for tea."

They didn't believe me! I was shocked at such cynicism and told them so.

"We've got nothing in for tea," said my mum, which piece of illogicality ended the discussion.

I was irritated by their cynicism, but not surprised. None of them was a real fisherman after all. And it did serve to warn me of similar reactions at school.

My friends were equally sceptical. "Oh yes, you got one. A ten pounder no doubt, like all those monsters you claim to catch in Ireland."

"No, it was only about a pound," I replied, defiant, but resenting having to defend my beautiful fish in front of these Philistines.

"I expect you had it stuffed and put in a glass case."

"No. I put it back."

They all nudged each other knowingly.

"Oh yeah! Right!"

"I did. Honest!"

"Gizza break Cluffy. Next time bring it home. We might believe you then."

All of which taught me another of life's little lessons. That fishing, at least as far as I am concerned, is a private business. What I do and what I catch are of interest only to me. I don't go fishing to impress people. Nor do I go fishing to indulge in competitions with other fishermen. Nor even to pretend to myself that I am a better fisherman than anyone else.

I am doing it because I derive great personal satisfaction from a sport which for me can never become boring. Fishing includes so many skills – fly tying, fly identification, river craft, casting, stalking - before you even come into contact with the supposed quarry, so that no two days can ever be the same. Catching the fish is pleasant, it can be exciting, but it is never an end in itself. There are days when just to be out on the river bank is enough.

If you doubt the truth of this last statement, try fishing where the fishing is really easy. One of those man-made ponds full of fat farm fish, hand-reared on pellets. Catch a trout with every cast and see how long it takes you before boredom sets in. Not long, I'll bet.

That's because you're not experiencing the many delights of real fishing. You're not having to out-think the fish. How can you out-think a fish which knows nothing about being a fish?

That is why I could never become a specimen hunter, or a match fisherman or a reservoir flogger. Each fish is precious and significant to me – not something to be recorded, weighed, or used for profit. Still less is fishing something that I need to do to accord me social status, as so many seem to view it nowadays.

Real fishermen are philosophers.

100 Perch

In Ireland the road from Clones to Newtownbutler appears to be an unremarkable road in almost every way. It begins its undistinguished journey in the centre of Clones, near Grandad Johnny's bicycle shop and the Creighton Hotel at the bottom of Fermanagh Street. It passes the bustling entrance to the railway station (a busy junction for several lines in the 1950s). From then on there is little of interest, a terrace of redbrick, a lengthy row of ordinary houses, a sense of leaving the town and entering open countryside. There is no reason for a casual visitor to pause more than a few moments on the Newtownbutler Road. It would remain quiet and almost unused, were it not for one thing. This is the road from Co Monaghan to Co Fermanagh. This is the road across the border.

A mile or so out of Clones town the Newtownbutler Road crosses the border to Northern Ireland. It leaves one country and enters another, very different country. At the border itself are two small buildings, one proclaiming itself in Irish to be the Eire border post, the one further along the road announcing in English that it is the Northern Ireland Customs post, and therefore part of Great Britain. For this is the border between two countries: the Republic of Ireland and the United Kingdom, and since its creation in 1922, has been the cause of much murder and mayhem.

Our Grandad, Johnny Gray, lived with his wife in one of the last houses in the Irish Republic, a house not half a mile from the border, the border that divided Ireland in two. Johnny was of no religious or political persuasion, except by accident of birth. He was born a Protestant, and to be a Protestant in the Irish Republic meant that your life was constantly at risk, because the militant Republicans of the IRA viewed them as enemy agents, pro-British invaders of their country. They wanted rid of them, and to that end were prepared to kill.

And it was here we came to stay with Grandad every summer in the 1950s.

Johnny lived with his second wife, a phenomenally mindless woman he had only recently married, while in his fifties. His first wife, our Grandma, had died suddenly in 1942, while still a young woman of only 43. His new wife's name was Lala, which we thought was hilarious, but indicative of her limited intelligence. She was a fussy, irritating woman, a firm believer in some extremely religious Protestant sect. None of us liked her.

Johnny himself was, to everyone's relief, entirely free of any strong religious feelings, and was a rarity in Ireland, being popular with both Protestants and Roman Catholics.

His house was very different from the houses back in Yorkshire, in England. It was very old, with a neat front garden, a garage and a huge back garden. This led to the woods and one of the many loughs that dotted the countryside around Clones.

The house was old-fashioned. There was no electricity for a start, which made every evening into an exciting adventure. Paraffin lamps were lit and we would sit and talk long into the night in near darkness, among the pleasant smell of the burning lamps, our faces lit only by the glow of the paraffin lights and the dried peat on the fire.

There was no real kitchen, all cooking being done on the huge iron 'range' in the main room. This black giant filled one wall, and had a variety of metal doors, leading to little ovens, big ovens, hotplates where a kettle always simmered, an open fire for cooking toast and a large hook which swung out so that pans could be attached. This range was constantly lit and it provided both heat and cooking facilities, as well as the unforgettably haunting smell of burning turf.

Not only was there no electricity or gas connected to the house, there was no water either. All water had to be collected in big metal jugs from the pump outside on the Newtownbutler road, a pump which was shared with the other nearby houses.

The walls of the house were attractively wood-panelled, in a dark, shiny wood. The floors were wooden too, just bare varnished boards. All this wood and varnish gave the house a warm, friendly feel and the scent of years long gone.

There were several oddities to the house (not counting Lala.) Downstairs, opposite the main room, was a doorway, a room we were never allowed to enter unaccompanied, a doorway which was usually kept locked, and into which no-one except Johnny, (who held the keys) was allowed access. This was Johnny's shrine to his beloved first wife, Lucinda Isabella, the mother of his three children, and our dead Grandma. Every day Johnny would open this door and disappear inside for an hour or more and when he emerged he would lock the door after him. We said nothing about these visits, as he always looked tearful for some time afterwards.

Then there was the budgie, Wee Tony. Wee Tony was Johnny's pride and joy and every evening the bird would be let out of his cage for a flight around the room. Having had his exercise, he would alight on Grandad's head, and the conversation would begin, for Wee Tony was no ordinary budgie able to chirp only a few words. Wee Tony was a PhD of the budgie world, for Wee Tony could hold a conversation, and understand what was being said. If truth was told, Wee Tony was probably more intelligent than Lala, and as a result Johnny and he would chat away to each other for an hour or more. It was hilarious.

Another oddity of Johnny's house was the toilet. There wasn't one, well, not in the house anyway. Outside in the garden was a wooden shed, a dark, loathsome place, without windows or light of any sort. Inside the shed you closed the door and felt your way in the dark to the toilet seat.

This was a large wooden board, with a hole in the middle. Here you sat and enjoyed the only pleasant part of the whole experience, for the wooden seat was warm and worn smooth by many years of bottom erosion. It was on this seat that all toilet business was to be done, a repulsive activity which we all postponed for as long as possible, only going outside when any further delay might prove disastrous.

A final oddity of Johnny's house was Lala's water barrel. This was a huge black wooden barrel, situated at the back of the house. All the rainwater which fell on the roof of the house drained into this barrel by a complicated series of pipes, so that it was constantly full and refreshed almost daily by the gentle Irish rain. A heavy lid kept the water clean and uncontaminated by birds. The barrel was Lala's prize possession, for this precious and pure rainwater was what she used to wash her hair.

Despite her extreme religious piety Lala was very vain about her hair, which was long and straight and grey. Bizarrely, she chose to wear these slate-grey tresses in a long ponytail, hoping perhaps to look like a teenage girl, ponytails being the fashion of the day. Far from looking youthful, the long grey hank of hair that hung down her back made her look from behind like an elderly grey mare. The resemblance didn't end there.

The point about this hair was that she obsessively washed it every day in the pure rainwater collected in the barrel. It was the main ritual of her day (because she did very little in the way of housework - cooking and cleaning not being her strengths.) However, she was very defensive and protective of her rainwater barrel, and no-one else was allowed to use her rainwater.

"Silly cow," said our Eck. "Let's pee in it."

And so it was that on one hot sunny day in 1958, two small boys, one aged eight and the other aged five, set off together for a day's fishing. Johnny was out at work in his bicycle shop. Lala was fussing about the house, being irritating as usual. Our parents had gone to visit some friends of our mothers at Killycronaghan. This was all quite normal. As kids we were allowed to roam free and wild all day long. No-one worried about us because no-one would bother us.

We took our tackle, two small spinning rods and two cheap and incredibly inefficient Intrepid spinning reels, our big red perch bungs, our bucketful of worms, and off we went walking together down the road towards the border.

We soon left the houses behind and entered the countryside. Here the land was well-farmed and fertile. Little cottages lay hidden among twisting lanes lined by tall hedges. There were tiny green fields with big hawthorn hedges full of wildlife. Birds called to each other, insects buzzed among the many flowers. In the roadside meadows, cows grazed contentedly or lay on their sides chewing slowly on the lush green grass.

It was a beautiful day and we happily made our way down the road, occasionally kicking up stones, until eventually we came to the Eire border post. The Guard was at the window of the wooden building, and when he saw us walking towards him, he came out to speak to us. (Irish police are called Guards, spelled Gardai in Irish.) He was a nice friendly man and was probably glad of someone to talk to.

He knew Johnny and so he was aware of who we were, Johnny's grandchildren.

"Hello there boys!" he called, and back into the customs shed he explained to someone, "It's just Johnny's wee boys."

He made a show of inspecting us for contraband (there was a lot of smuggling going on in those days, because of the large difference in prices of many goods between the North and South.) He wanted to know if we had any pigs hidden away. It was all just a joke.

The inspection over, he waved us on our way. "Hope you catch some big wuns boys!" he called.

It was on to the next Customs Post, the British one, where the ritual was repeated. Here too we were known.

"Johnny told everyone you were coming for the summer," said the Customs man. He let us through with a pat on the head.

We were nearly there.

Our destination was a little stream that meandered along the border hereabouts, crisscrossing it several times. Sometimes the stream was an Irish stream, and sometimes it was a British stream. It never seemed to make any difference to the fishing, which was just sublime.

This stream was surprisingly deep and crystal clear and incredibly fertile, yet never more than about four feet wide. The banks were lined with tall reeds and even some bulrushes. Beautiful water lilies sprouted everywhere in the slow-moving water, their white leaves cupping golden insides.

This little stream was full of the fiercest, fattest perch

we had ever seen. We'd discovered them the year before, and ever since then had dreamed of returning. Now the great day had finally come.

We settled down in the grass, among the purple and white clover and the yellow buttercups, and baited our hooks. Little did we realise that this was to be a day neither of us would ever forget.

I helped our Eck bait his hook, and cast out for him, with just a gentle flick into the clear water. I aimed to land the bait as near to the waterlily pads as possible. I knew that the perch liked to live among the fronds of the water lilies, so they could dive back in amongst them for protection, should a vicious old pike come along.

The red float settled quickly, sitting up nice and straight with only the red top showing. This meant that I had set the float at the right depth and the bait was free of the bottom. It sailed very slowly down the stream, for the water moved barely perceptibly and ever so quietly through these verdant meadows.

Satisfied that everything was going well, I started to pass the rod over to our Eck. He held out both hands to take it, but had only just got hold of the butt when the float started bobbing.

"Look! It's a bite!" I called.

He clicked the bar of the reel over to lock the line. The float was bouncing, bouncing.

"It's gone under Eck! Strike!"

He struck and the fish was on! It dived for the depths, pulling hard and taking the float with it. We could tell immediately that it was a perch because of the fierce fight it gave, bouncing, bouncing the rod up and down. Rudd don't fight like that.

Eck held on tight, and fought the fish with a great happy grin on his face.

"Keep it down, don't make too much of a splash, it'll scare the others," I urged.

He did as he was told, and steered the fish into the side, lifting it up to our sight very gently.

There it was on the surface, a big bright wriggling perch, with bold black stripes on its silver body, startlingly red fins, and a sharp-looking dorsal fin, raised in anger.

"Pass it over here," I said, excited at such a quick catch and the sight of such a beautiful fish.

He brought the perch within reach. It glared indignantly at us, as if astonished to be out of the water. Quickly, I seized the line and beached the fish onto the grass, kneeling and carefully taking hold, very wary of those spiky sharp points on its dorsal fin. A quick twist of the hook and it came free. He had only lip-hooked it, so there was no damage to the fish.

"There!" I held it up for him to see. "Well done our kid!"

Eck grinned happily. "First cast! It took straight away!"

He leaned forward and touched it gently with the tip of one finger. "What a beauty!"

"Yep! I'll put it back now."

I leaned close to the water's edge and tipped the perch out of my hands.

"One nil!" he said.

I laughed. He could be very competitive, our kid.

I re-baited his hook and this time left it to him to re-cast. I wanted to be fishing myself, not spending the day unhooking his catches!

As the day had begun successfully, so it continued. The morning passed in a mad hectic frenzy of bobbing floats, of striking and hooking, of bending rods and fighting fish. We were catching fish every cast, and not just tiddlers. 'Striddly boys' as Grandad called them.

These were fierce fighting perch, in perfect condition and of amazing size for such a small stream. Most of them were over nine inches long, and some were monsters – great heavy fish of a pound or more. Each one we caught we unhooked carefully and returned to the stream.

What was even more amazing than the quality and size of the fish was that the fish never went off the boil, seizing our worms with ferocity for the whole of the morning and then all the afternoon, so that eventually we had to ration our worms. Even though we had started with a big bucketful of them the fish were taking so frequently and so violently that we were in danger of running out. Instead of changing worms after each fish, we had to retain the same used worm, and re-cast.

The afternoon passed without us noticing the time, as the whole experience was so intoxicating. Bait the hook, cast the line, watch the float. Bobbing, bobbing, it's gone under! Strike! Don't let it get into the reeds or the lilies. Steer it clear, swing it ashore. Unhook, rebait, recast… we never tired of the excitement.

At some point I had to say, "Just use half a worm or we'll run out."

We did go on to use only half worms, and still these fantastic perch kept taking them as frenetically as ever. Often we both had fish on at the same time, running up and down the banks trying to avoid getting tangled with each other.

"They'll take anything!" I yelled.

"They'd probably eat us if we fell in!"

We laughed and landed our fish and cast out again.

"Another one!"

"I've got one too!"

"My God, this is brilliant our kid!"

"They're Piranha Perch!"

By the end of the afternoon we had caught over a hundred of them in one single day. When we ran out of worms, we cast in our lines with bare hooks, and we still caught fish. I can remember it vividly even now, sixty years later.

A hundred perch. What a day it was.

Nor was that the end of the fun and games. We had kept a few of the smaller perch in the empty worm bucket, which we half-filled with water to keep them alive.

Eck had a plan.

We walked home along the road to the border and back towards Co Monaghan. The customs men came out to see how we had got on with the fishing, and we showed them the fish. Then we walked back up the Newtownbutler road all the way to Grandad's house.

And there we ended our unforgettable day, by tipping the perch into Lala's water barrel.

Fivemiletown

Grandad Johnny had three children, our Ma, her sister Aunt Peggy in Co Cavan, and a son, our Uncle Jack, who lived just over the border in the North, where he had a garage and a farm. We often went to stay with him and his family in Fivemiletown, a little town in Co Tyrone on the other side of the mystical mountain called Slieve Beagh. Although it was named Five mile town it wasn't actually five miles from anywhere, being six from Brookeborough, seven from Clogher, eight from Tempo and nine from Fintona. This was the sort of whimsical oddity that made me love Ireland.

We spent many happy hours fishing around the area, for this too was a wonderful land of rivers and lakes, which even in peaceful times were largely unfished. The lakes – or loughs - were nearly all coarse fishing, for perch, rudd (called roach locally) and pike, though there were some dark still waters where odd Irish varieties of trout lurked in unimaginable depths.

Lough Erne, nearby, was a huge water system, one of the biggest in the whole of the British Isles, containing rivers, loughs and channels which absolutely teemed with fish. Hundred pound catches in a day were commonplace. The density of fish in these waters was just amazing to anyone accustomed to fishing the scant and impoverished waters that were the usual fare for anglers in much of England.

I fished with young local lads at Lisnaskea, hauling shoals of huge bream out of Lough Erne, bream that most anglers in England could only dream of catching, and yet here the youngsters thought nothing of it, little realising how lucky they were to be fishing an angling paradise.

The rivers around Fivemiletown were mostly trout fishing. There were no grayling in Ireland and few real river roach as in England. The only other fish you might catch in the rivers were salmon, or salmon parr, annoying little parodies of real salmon.

Most of the rivers drained into the Erne system, the Colebrooke River being the main one of these, a stony-bottomed river about the size of the Nidd back home in Yorkshire. It had some lovely fast runs, some quiet shady stretches under trees and one or two really big dark holes. There were many rivers of this type, flowing through meadowland and small woods. Trout in them were rarely more than a pound and half, but they provided good fly fishing or upstream worming.

In some valleys there was a very different type of river, small, deep and fertile, flowing gently through boggy fields. The bed of these rivers was mostly silt, providing a sleepy, slow-moving little stream, meandering through meadows where the only visitors were mooching cattle.

Often these little rivers contained a surprise or two for the angler – for their fertility fed the fish so well they could attain heavy weights. My friend Noel Mills pulled a four pound trout out of a pool under a bridge, where the river was so narrow I could jump across it.

These lovely little rivers were, however, often devilish hard to fish. They were so fertile that they were full of weed from May onwards, so it was usually a case of lowering a worm into a comparatively weed-free hole, (if you could find one) and hoping for the best.

And finally, there were the moorland rivers up on the hills, on the sides of the mountain called in Irish Slieve Beagh. This was the border between the North and the South, a wild land of myths and legends. Here the fishing was upland in style, like the becks back home in the upper reaches of the Nidd and the Wharfe. The land was poor, there was little food for the fish, so the trout were small and hungry and fierce. The water was brown and peat-stained, and looked just like tea. You were in an ancient and almost uninhabited country, and it felt like it.

As if the river fishing wasn't enough, there were the loughs to try as well. In Fivemiletown there were two loughs – the 'town' lough, which had a cleared and domesticated area for swimming and diving – which anyone could fish for free; and the lough in the estate of Blessingbourne, which was supposedly private property.

The one big trouble with fishing the Irish loughs was that most of them were very difficult to access. They were invariably surrounded by wet bogland, for there was very little firm land in the central counties of Ireland. This bogland was often green and apparently solid, but underneath was a sodden mass of dangerous black mud and water, and this was a potential deathtrap for the unwary. It was very risky to wade into the reeds at the side of a lough, because you could easily fall into a deep hole, or get your boots stuck and be unable to escape the clutching mud.

Even when it was possible to reach the water's edge, there was quite probably another fifteen yards of tall reeds and bulrushes between the fisherman and truly open water. Beyond the reeds there would be another five or ten yards of thick lily pads, which really added to the fisherman's problems. These lily pads were attached to very strong and thick stems under the water, on which light tackle would inevitably snag and break.

Because of all these difficulties it was obvious that there was a great premium placed on fishable water. Either you had to have a boat (which was surprisingly rare in Ireland) or you went and fished from the landing stage in the town lough, or you sneaked into the private Blessingbourne estate and fished illegally from their boathouse.

The town lough was (and still is) a large lake right on the edge of the town. Down the Main street and just a couple of hundred yards past the Orange Hall there was the turnoff into the woods and the lough. It was a lovely, unspoiled lake, fringed with a ring of bulrushes, tall reeds and lily pads as usual, and with open fields on three sides.

The town council had made several attempts to turn the lough into an amenity, by clearing an area of reeds and creating a swimming pool for kids. There was a concreted area, with two solid-looking changing rooms, benches for the adults to sit on, and best of all, a long jetty leading out to a diving board. This was a solid wooden structure, built of wood on stilts above the water. And from this diving board it was possible to fish, as the weeds and bulrushes had been cleared sufficiently to leave a wide weed-free area.

Here Eck and I spent many happy hours, usually in the company of Noel Mills, the son of the publican of The Chestnut Bar, a lad of my own age, a keen fisherman and a real character.

The fishing we did there was pretty basic – big red perch bungs and either worms or bread paste. The fish were plentiful – usually big fat perch on the worms, or lovely golden rudd on the bread paste. The excitement was always there, because although you never knew what you might catch, you were certain that once the float went under you had a fierce fighting fish on the other end!

There was spinning too, for this cleared area was the only part of the whole lough which was free enough of weeds to spin. Everywhere else you would be entangled in the water lilies and tall reeds. Spinning brought plenty of jack pike and an occasional perch, but rarely a big pike.

All this variety of fishing just around Fivemiletown was amazing and all of it free and wild. It was rare indeed to meet another angler. There were no well-trodden riverbank paths, no crowds, no litter, no carparks. I always laugh when I see fishermen in England fly fishing on reservoirs, spaced out at intervals every few yards, and I think wrily of 'going fishing to get away from it all.'

Around Clones there were at least sixty loughs, and a few miles away in County Cavan, where my Aunt Peggy and my other cousins lived, there were 365 loughs, one for every day of the year. All of this fishing was completely free.

In Irish fishing too there was always an element of surprise, which you didn't often get on the tamed waters of England. If you fished on the Trent or the Severn, you knew exactly what was on offer. Not in Ireland. The fish there were totally wild fish, not stocked or reared on a fish farm. They grew just as big as the food supply and the predators would allow, and in the virtual absence of the worst predator of the lot – Man – they could attain huge sizes.

On Irish waters you never knew what you might pull out.

The Dripping Dog

It was a cold winter's day in Yorkshire. I was ten and my brother, our Eck, was seven. It was in that slack period just after Christmas, when all the presents have been opened and played with and everyone was feeling just a little bored. There were a few days yet to the thrills of staying up late on New Year's Eve, so what were we going to do? The weather was grim and grey, but what had our dad got in store for us?

"Let's go fishing!" said our dad.

Our Ma rolled her eyes heavenward. "Have you looked out of the window?"

A gale was howling across the icy landscape. Grey frost rimed the trees. There was no bird or animal life to be seen.

Dad dismissed her fears. "Bit of fresh air never hurt anyone. Get your coats on boys."

Poor Ma, she was so used to his enthusiasms that she bore them with a phlegmatic spirit. No she didn't, she went ballistic.

"Talk sense man! Fishing in this weather?"

"Perfect for fishing," he answered blithely.

"You're a bloody eejit! They'll catch their death of cold out there!"

Dad ignored her. "David, you go and dig some worms. I'll get some sandwiches made."

He glanced towards our Ma. "They'll soon warm you up."

Half an hour later and we were in the car. Ma had

stayed at home, refusing to have anything to do with this 'eejit trip'. At this juncture we need to make a few points about our dad.

Despite being the son of George Henry, one of the best fishermen in the district, our Dad was in truth not a real fisherman at all. He had the enthusiasm and the desire, but sadly he was entirely deficient in the angling skills required to land a fish. It was a mystery I was unable to solve until late in his life. Nevertheless, this lack of angling skills did not prevent him taking us fishing.

Our Dad, known as Happy Harry to one and all, was an inventive man, a man full of bright ideas, and this particular day, his bright idea was to go fishing. His technique in life was to follow his enthusiasms, particularly ones fuelled by a bright idea.

Today he was bored of being stuck in the house and he wanted a change of scenery. Hence the bright idea – a day on the river. He had decided he wanted to go fishing with his two boys, so regardless of the freezing conditions outside, we were going fishing. He collected the sandwiches and his proudest fishing possession, a rod licence that had expired three years earlier.

So we hadn't got a legitimate licence, we hadn't got any fishing permits, not even a day ticket, but what did it matter, we were going fishing!

Dad drove us to Boroughbridge seven miles away. Boroughbridge, as its name suggests, is an historic town built around the bridge over the River Ure. Here the Ure is in its lower reaches and is a mighty river, so for centuries the bridge has been an important crossing point, the only one for many miles around.

Above the bridge there is a massive weir, over which the river pours with spectacular violence. Running up alongside the weir there is a salmon ladder, a series of level watery pools, built in the days when the Ure had a run of salmon. Beside the river there is also a canal, so as a fishing spot it offers a lot of variety.

We parked away from the town, over the bridge, in a little car park on the island at the junction of the river and canal. Dad turned the engine off and we looked out at the chilly scene. There in front of us was the river, roaring along in a brown foam-flecked flood. It was about a hundred yards across. Anyone falling in the water would be instantly swept away to an icy death.

Inside the car we sat glumly still. No-one wanted to leave the warmth.

Dad was the first to move. "Well come on lads!" he said brightly. "We've come all this way. Let's get fishing!"

He opened the door to an icy blast that nearly tore the door off its hinges.

Our Eck had to be prised out of the car, clinging onto the seats while protesting violently, until Dad dragged him outside.

Dad marched us up the narrow spit of island between the canal and the river, to where the island reached a point. Beyond this we could not go. On one side of us was the river, admittedly a bit calmer here because it was upstream of the mighty weir. On the other side of the island was the canal, deep and black and uninviting. There was some slight shelter from the wind provided by the tree cover, so it was here that Dad pitched camp.

No-one else was out and about on such a cold day. Everyone else had more sense than our dad. There were a few frozen-looking mallard huddling in the decaying reeds of the canal side. Something white and birdlike was hiding in the undergrowth. It might have been a seagull, it might have been a penguin. It was certainly cold enough for the latter.

We tackled up. Float-fishing worms. As everyone except my dad knew, this was a useless method of fishing, which would only catch the occasional fish, an old chub perhaps, a chub tired of life, or maybe an ancient trout driven by hunger and malnutrition into taking such a sucker bait.

We caught nothing.

We fished for two hours. Two miserable shivering hours. It was so cold my fingers couldn't manipulate the handle on the reel. I gave up trying, leaving the useless float lying there dead in the water, not caring if we caught a fish or died of frostbite.

We sat together in silence, a silence broken only by my dad's enthusiastic cries, "I think I've got a bite!" (He never had.) We ignored him.

By lunchtime we were cold, dispirited and hungry. We were all looking forward to some food, preferably hot food which would fill us up and warm our depressed spirits. Our Eck was beginning to look rebellious.

"I'm starving," he announced.

Dad nodded understandingly. He delved into a big bag. Seeing this, our hopes rose. We put down our rods and eagerly anticipated what goodies might be coming our way.

"Here you are boys! Lovely grub!"

He handed Eck and me a paper-wrapped packet each.

Eck looked suspiciously at his. "What's this?"

"A sandwich."

Eck opened the paper and sniffed the bread. "What sort of sandwich?"

Dad looked away, an evasive movement I noticed with suspicion.

Eck persisted. "Dad? What's in the sandwiches?" He was not to be ignored.

"Dripping," Dad said brightly, adding quickly, "It's very good for you. Eat up."

Dripping, for those who have never heard of such delights, is fat. Pure, unadulterated beef fat, made from the boiled-down carcass of a bullock. It is totally disgusting, incredibly unhealthy, and incidentally is not the sort of food you need to eat when you are sitting on a freezing riverbank at the end of December with a total madman.

Our kid went crazy.

"Dripping! It's disgusting! I'm not eating Dripping!"

"Get it down you. It'll warm you up!"

"No it won't!" Eck threw down his sandwich and danced with rage. "I'm not eating it! Not ever! So there!"

Dad rose to his feet. "There's nothing else. Eat it up."

"No!"

"Eat it up. Or you'll starve." (Cunning psychology was not a strongpoint with our Dad.)

At that moment something furry intruded. It was a dog, a scruffy hairy dog, snuffling at my face. A lonesome, hungry dog without an owner.

"Hello dog," I said. The dog did not reply.

Dad pointed at the Dripping sandwich. "Eat it up or I'll give it to the dog." (Not a tactic to use with our kid, I guessed.)

Eck stood there defiantly.

"Go on then. Give it to him. I bet he won't eat it."

Dad patted the dog's head. "You want it doggie? You can have it!"

He picked up the sandwich and fed it to the dog, who wolfed it down with apparent delight.

"See!" said our dad. "He loves it!"

Eck gave our dad a look of utter contempt. "It's a dog dad. It'll eat anything."

By this time the dog had wolfed down the entire Dripping sandwich, two thick slices of bread with a great big wodge of slimy grey fat between them. Amazingly, he seemed to like Dripping. He grinned, looking at each of us in turn, clearly hoping for more.

Then the grey fatty mass must have hit his stomach. The dog grimaced, and let out a howl. A terrible, piercing, unearthly howl.

Aghast, we stood and watched as the dog howled his long and unhappy howl, then, without warning, it turned and ran to the icy river and, without stopping, launched itself furiously into the flood.

We were all horrified at this unexpected outcome, none more so than our Eck.

"See what you've done now! Poisoned the dog with your Dripping sandwiches!"

It seemed there was nothing we could do to save the poor mutt from drowning. The dog, plainly unsettled by the unusual contents of its stomach, was trying vainly to swim across the raging river. The water was freezing, the current far too strong for him, so unless we could somehow rescue it, the poor animal would surely die.

"It's all your fault!" Eck shouted at Dad. "You

murderer!"

We rushed to the riverside and began to call to the dog.

"Here doggie!"

"Good doggie!"

"Come back here doggie!"

It was no use. The dog, probably suffering from cold-water shock by now, was insensible to our cries, and, no doubt suffering pangs of pain from its diet of Dripping, continued to try to battle the current. In seconds it had left the shelter of the bank and had been swept away in the surging brown torrent.

"Oh my God!" said Dad, who in truth was a kindly soul who would never wish any animal to come to harm.

The three of us ran, stumbling, shouting and panicking, along the riverbank, desperately trying to coax the poor dog ashore. It was only fifty yards more to the weir and if the dog was swept over that the poor animal would stand no chance in the boiling waters below.

We hurried along to prevent this happening, and by some miracle we reached the weir before the poor beast. There we stood, helplessly shouting at the drowning dog. The noise we were making brought some people out of their cars to see what was happening.

Luckily for us, the current suddenly swung the helpless creature in towards our bank and miraculously the dog was swept into shore and safety. His feet could be seen paddling slowly with his last few gasps of energy.

Some more people now appeared, standing watching our antics without comment. Quite a crowd had gathered.

Dad rushed to the river's edge and called, "Here Doggie, here!"

Luckily, the dog didn't seem to recognise our dad as the maniac who had poisoned him, and it staggered ashore, shivering uncontrollably. Dad rushed to the dog and with a great show of affection, wrapped his arms lovingly around it. Then he cradled the bedraggled dog in his arms and lifted it up the banking.

The watchers, now swelled to a crowd of a dozen or so, watched in disapproving silence.

Dad carried the dog through the crowd to our car, and as he did so I heard a loud voice from among the watchers.

"Funny thing to do, letting the dog swim in the river at this time of year."

Dad pretended not to hear the criticism. He opened the car boot and took out an old blanket, rubbing the dog down with fierce but very affectionate movements, while whispering loving comments in its ear. Slowly the dog recovered.

Our hearts were pounding, our minds reeling with the thought that we were nearly responsible for the death of the poor animal, an animal that had trusted us to feed it something edible, and not a highly-toxic Dripping sandwich. Not only that, there were plenty of witnesses to our Dad's criminality and cruelty.

Avoiding the hostile stares of the crowd, our Dad patted the dog and put it down.

"Get in the car boys." He glanced at the crowd. "Quickly now."

In silence, we packed the rods into the boot.

Dad gave the dog a final affectionate pat on the head and shooed it away from the car.

No-one spoke all the way home.

As we parked outside our house our dad leant close to our Eck and in a low, but very insistent voice said, "Not a word about this to your mother. Understand?"

Our Eck grinned. "What's it worth?"

He knew that he had a secret hold over his father, a hold that would one day come in useful.

Dad whispered something in his ear, and our Eck nodded.

As we were about to enter the kitchen door, he tugged at his dad's arm and hissed, "Remember you owe me. Murderer!"

Blessingbourne

In total contrast to our miserable fishing at home, Ireland in the 1950s was truly a fisherman's paradise. There were thousands of loughs, most of them rarely fished and many of them never fished. There were pike so strong that they could pull you into the water, bream the size of dustbin lids, beautiful red and gold rudd, fierce fighting perch and trout the size of tuna. And it was all free!

In the Blessingbourne estate at Fivemiletown there were actually three loughs – a large one and two smaller interconnected feeder loughs. The largest lough was in front of an imposing house, the home of local dignitaries. The rule as long as I had known the place was that the owners were very generous and didn't mind people fishing in their loughs, so long as they didn't fish from the lawns in front of the house, or from the boathouse.

Unfortunately, this was the one cleared area of the whole lough, and so it was to the boathouse that we invariably went, though in twenty years of fishing there I could only remember being ejected once, and that in the most polite and mild terms. Can you imagine such generosity in England? I doubt it.

The boathouse was an old wooden affair, built into the banks of the lough. Entry was gained via a low back door. Once inside, there was a rowing boat tethered by a rope and space for two fishermen to stand, each one clinging to an outside wall and wading carefully in the water, until the open front of the boathouse was reached.

Obviously, we weren't allowed to use the boat, so there you stood – one fisherman on each side of the boathouse entrance – each fisherman balanced precariously in the water, with it reaching almost to the top of his wellington boots. A dangerous place to fish from, but one worth every risk. In front of the boathouse was clear water, clear fishable water, water full of pike that dreams are made of, for the pike in Blessingbourne were beasts.

The water was so fertile and warm, so full of weed and aquatic life, that it supported a vast head of perch and rudd. The pike fed on these and in the virtual absence of their only enemy – fishermen – they attained great size and weight.

At this date I had landed no real monsters, but I had hooked pike which were the size of freshwater sharks. These beasts had so far eluded capture, for the problem at Blessingbourne was not the hooking of such great fish, the real difficulty was getting them landed out of the weed and lilypad-laced water.

Let's go back in time. Ireland was at peace, the country was prospering, most people had no time for 'that oul nonsense'. The summer was warm and dry and Noel Mills and I were creeping through the rhododendron bushes of Blessingbourne gardens, hoping to scurry across the next twenty yards of clear ground to reach the boathouse without being seen from the big house.

We were eleven years old. We both had a tin of worms, and Noel in addition had a packet of ten Gallahers Reds he'd stolen from his father's Chestnut Bar. We were all set for a great day's fishing.

We each carried two rods already tackled up. I had a long twelve-foot steel rod (my trusty Accles and Pollock, bought on HP for a few bob per week). This had a 3lb line, a red perch bung and a size 12 hook for use with dough or worms, and this was to be used to catch our live bait. The other rod was a short powerful one, a stocky six-foot fibreglass pike-tamer, with a massive pike bung, two feet of thick steel trace and a bloody great treble hook – for use when we'd caught our livebait.

There are some I know who decry this method, saying it is cruel. All I can say is, Nature is cruel. The three or four rudd Noel and I would use in a day were as nothing compared to the hundreds being killed each day by the pike. Or worse still, the millions of fish killed world-wide by manmade poisons, plastics and pollution.

Noel was a chubby cheery lad, possessed of an amazing vocabulary of technicolour obscenity. Here at Blessingbourne however, we were silent, having no need to talk. We knew what we were here for and we knew how to do it. Crouching low to avoid detection, we ran as fast as we could to the boathouse. Once there, we dropped onto our knees and ducked inside the low roof of the building.

Inside it was wonderfully quiet and still. There was the gentle lapping of wavelets against the wooden walls. Reflected light made wave patterns on the roof as the sun shone through the open front of the boathouse. The air smelled of old, warm wood. In front of us was the lough, open, tempting and cleared of bulrushes and weed.

There was the tethered rowing boat, rocking softly on its moorings. Noel looked enviously at it.

"Jeezus! What I'd give for a fockin ride in that fockin yoke!" (a yoke was a vehicle of any sort.)

It was a temptation, but quite out of the question, for they'd see us from the big house and we'd be in trouble. Still, a boat would have made fishing a lot easier.

Noel climbed into the boat.

"Don't Noel!"

"Ach, fock off! I'm not rowing the fockin boat!"

He was trying to get over to the far wall, so he could perch on the end stanchion to fish.

The boat wallowed with his considerable weight, slapping waves against the walls and threatening us with discovery.

"Sssh! They'll hear us!"

Noel stopped, held his breath, and we both listened for sounds indicating we had been seen. Nothing. The waves subsided. No-one was coming.

We were both wearing wellies, being unable to afford such luxuries as waders, which would probably have been dangerous anyway, as the bottom of the lough was soft clinging mud. If we'd fallen in with waders on, we'd probably never have got out again.

Through the open front of the boathouse we could see the lough - flat calm, warm in the sun, with blue dragonflies buzzing about among the yellow and white waterlily flowers. Ah, were there ever such times as these!

To reach the fishing positions at the front was not easy – we had to put our rods into the boat and edge along the walls, holding onto the supporting timbers. If either of us slipped we would be straight into three feet of water and the silty bottom of the lough. There was only an inch or two between the surface of the water and the tops of our wellies. There was no room for rapid movements or for any clowning about.

Eventually we were both in position, perched delicately on the square foot of concrete piling at the base of each front doorpost. Then we pulled the boat towards us, each teetering on his own footing, to retrieve the rods.

The plan was simple – to use the long rods first in order to catch the livebait, then, when we were ready, to bait up the pike rods for the real action – the battle with the Beasts of Blessingbourne.

Livebait was ideally a silvery rudd about six inches long (how I detest that wretched French millimetre rubbish. The Yanks kept their inches, why couldn't we?) Six inches long was just perfect.

Everything of course had to be done quietly and carefully, in case we were caught trespassing. There must be no yelling out if we got a fish, or more likely, if we fell in.

Suddenly, before we'd even started, there was a splash and an alarming rattle of reeds in the water, not five yards from where we stood. Pike.

I mouthed to Noel. "Did you see that?"

He nodded.

A big pike was close inshore. This might be a good sign for us (the pike were feeding and were close to us) or a bad sign (if pike were in this close to us they might have scared all the precious rudd away.) I preferred to think only that the pike were ravenously hungry.

The lough looked good today. I felt lucky. The omens were with me. We were going to catch something big.

Float fishing on a calm sunny day was always fun. I loved it. I set the float three feet deep to start with, then threaded a maggot-shaped lump of dough round the hook and cast out gently to a spot about ten yards away, just wide of some lily pads. I had this feeling that young rudd liked to linger among the lily fronds, able to dodge quickly out of sight of feeding pike.

I didn't have to wait long. My float bounced once,

twice. Noel grinned and concentrated on his own float, some distance to the right of mine.

The red float bobbed again. My lucky colour, I thought. Just one more nibble and I'd strike. (My favourite fishing book was of course *Mr Crabtree Goes Fishing.* I always used to expect a bubble to appear in the sky above me saying, "STRIKE PETER, STRIKE!")

Ploop. It vanished. I struck and felt the pull of a fish. A vigorous, bouncing tugging sort of fight.

"It's a perch."

Noel made a sour face. It was indeed a perch. About ten inches long, bright red-finned and black and white-striped. I wet my hands, unhooked it quickly and slid it back into the water. It was too big for live-baiting and anyway, we preferred rudd (or roach as Noel called them), our theory being that the big spines on a perch's dorsal fin put the pike off eating them, whereas a lovely soft silvery little rudd …… mmmm, a veritable delicacy for a hungry pike.

My next two were also perch, which was annoying. Normally rudd took the dough, the perch usually going for worms. Then Noel, who had so far caught nothing, changed his depth and was immediately into rudd. You could tell the difference straight away; rudd don't have the fierce tugging bite that even little perch have. Rudd are much gentler fish.

"Gotcha, ye wee hoor!" Noel grinned, unhooking the silvery bar from his hook. This added urgency to my fishing, for already Noel was baiting up his pike rod with his rudd.

I watched enviously as he leaned to his right, swung the line out, and hurled the tackle far out into the lough. There was an almighty splash – the bung – followed by a smaller, slapping sound – the live-bait. The rings they made in the water sent the lily pads rocking, then spread far over the placid reaches of the lough. I watched them, fascinated to see how far they would travel. A duck flew off, quacking loudly at the disturbance.

Quiet returned.

Noel's rudd was still alive after its flight, circling the bung, stirring it slightly and turning it round. It was easy to tell the difference when a pike took the bait – whoof! The bung would slide under and vanish as the pike sailed off with its prey.

"Your float's under, ye dozy eejit!"

I'd been so busy watching his pike bung that I'd missed a bite on my own rod. I struck, but was too late. The dough had gone. Noel sighed for my stupidity. I wound in and tried again.

Where the hell were they today? Normally it was a simple task to get half a dozen rudd, now, on this lucky day of all days, I couldn't get the hold of one measly rudd to livebait with.

Noel, who had re-tackled his rudd rod, called jeeringly, "I'll get ye wan if ye like, Englishman!"

He re-cast.

Cravenly, I half-wanted him to catch one for me, so I too could fish for pike, but the other half of me, the proud half, rejected such a patronising offer. If I couldn't catch a rudd for myself, then so be it. Fate would take its course.

Noel lit up a Gallaher's Red, inhaled deeply, and grinned at me, slowly blowing out an expert ring of smoke.

I sat proudly for ten minutes, my rudd float not stirring.

The pike we'd heard in the nearby shallows must have scared the little rudd away from my side of the boathouse. It could sometimes happen like this, I reflected - all my carefully-laid plans for pike-fishing ruined, and all because of the one thing that I hadn't considered a possibility, that I should fail to catch some bait.

I seethed in annoyance, and told myself that this should be a lesson to me. In future I should not be overconfident, that I should plan for every contingency, no matter how unlikely.

I wound in, changed my bait, and dropped my float a foot. Another bite. Another disappointment. Another perch. And just to add further irony, a perch who might have been a contender for the smallest rod-caught perch in the history of Irish fishing.

"Ah, a dacent fish at last!" grinned Noel, who was laughing at my miniscule perch.

I re-baited and re-cast and sat and waited.

In the sky the clouds were high over the trees on the far shore. There was a perfect reflection of them in the still water.

Noel grunted and pointed to his pike bung. It had stopped moving. Either the rudd was dead, or a pike had just swallowed it and was digesting his food. Noel quietly dropped his float rod into the boat, and gripped the butt of his pike rod tightly. He waited expectantly for the next move.

Whoof! The big red bung slid off under the water, heading away from us with the power of a train. Noel lifted his rod, ready to strike.

"Wait!" I counselled needlessly.

Noel gave me a reproving stare. He knew better than to

strike too soon. Let the pike run, then…………

Mr Crabtree's "STRIKE PETER, STRIKE!" appeared in the sky above the trees. Noel spat out his fag, firmly lifted his rod, clicked the bar of his reel over to engage, and slowly began winding up the slack.

Across the water the arc of his line tightened as the fish continued to draw away, then, when the line was almost straight, Noel lifted the rod and pulled back sharply, hopefully driving the hooks home in the hard bony mouth of a monster pike.

I looked nervously at him. Sometimes a pike would take the bait, but would only be holding the fish lightly in his jaws, not inside his mouth, so that when the angler struck the hooks weren't driven home. When that happened the pike could still sail away, as this one was doing now – but of course it wouldn't be hooked and could drop the bait at any time.

"Noel, is it on?"

"Course it is!" He let his cool pose drop, grinning widely. The rod was juddering as the pike shook its head angrily. "He's on! I've got the focker!"

"Ssssh! They'll hear us!"

"Shush be focked!"

Hurriedly, I wound in my float line to avoid getting our lines tangled when he brought his pike in. Then I pulled Noel's own float rod out of the way too. In my haste I slid off my pedestal. My boot filled with water as I overstretched, but there was no time to worry about a wet leg, we had a monster out there!

I grabbed our old half-torn net (we couldn't afford a better one and scorned to use so cruel an instrument as a gaff.) I crouched, ready to help Noel land his beast.

The fish, rather stupidly, had fought to gain the open

water, instead of heading into the reeds, where it might have snagged the line and broken free. Instead, Noel now had every advantage. He didn't waste time, quickly drawing the pike in after its two initial powerful surges.

I always love that time when you have something on the line, but you haven't yet seen what it is, or how big it is. You peer closely at the water, following the line into the depths, searching for a sight of……

"Fockin Jeezus!"

A sight of who knows what. There was a flash of white from the pike's belly, a white-spotted green flank as it sailed in towards us.

"What a fockin fish!"

It was enormous, a great fat green shark over a yard in length.

"Five pounds!" I said.

Noel had a secret Omen, that he should always drastically underestimate the size of his fish. I was only kidding when I said five pounds, for it was obvious this was no wee jack pike! This was a Beast!

Suddenly it saw us and swerved off to the left, splashing violently to the surface.

"Houly God! Look at the fockin size of that!"

Noel had been overconfident and now the fish was disturbing everything on the lough as it fought its way into the reeds. He had to pull hard to one side to get its head out of the rushes. It was boy against pike, a trial of strength, a battle Noel slowly began to win.

This second time the pike came in quietly, all the fight seemingly gone out of him. I got the net out ready and slid it into the water. The pike sailed slowly into the net. It was so huge the net only covered its head!

"Careful now!"

Desperately, I tried to draw the net over more of its body, but to my horror the fish slipped through the torn gap between the net and the rim.

Noel howled in dismay.

Luckily the pike was unaware of the problem. Noel said a world record number of obscene words in two seconds and swung the fish round for another attempt.

This time there was no mistake, and the fish sank into the net, a great fat meaty curve of green and white pike.

"Gottim!" I roared, as excited as Noel was now. My heart was pounding and I couldn't take my eyes off the beast, for it was over three feet long and as fat and round as a tuna fish.

Then, unbelievably, just as we struggled and lifted him and the net into the boat, the hooks fell right out of his mouth.

"Fockin Jasus!" Noel howled as the fish fell free into the boat. "Get the fockin fish!"

In his desperation he leaped into the boat to grab the pike, and as he did so everything seemed in go into slow motion. The boat tilted over with his weight, the gunwales slid into the water, which gushed over into the boat in torrents. We both watched in horror as the boat started to fill with water, and in seconds the lough lay open for the fish to sail away, unhooked, out of the net, completely without hindrance. It was free to go!

Amazingly, for some seconds the pike lay there unmoving inside the now half-submerged boat, not realizing it was unhooked and free to escape.

I stared at it, as ever half afraid. Pike always seemed to

have a smile on their faces, a wicked, greedy, wolfish smile. They're handsome brutes though, their flanks beautifully mottled and camouflaged. And what a shape for a fish eater. A toothed torpedo.

Noel waved desperately to me. He'd fallen in the water up to his waist. "Any chance of a hand here! I'm fockin drownin!"

I was still staring, mesmerized by the immense size of the thing. It was by far the biggest fish I had ever seen.

"What are ye gawpin at? Net the fockin fish will ye!"

I grabbed for the net, but to my horror, the pike suddenly realised it was no longer captured but was free and able to leave. With a casual wave of its tail, it swam slowly out of the boat and headed for freedom and there was nothing we could do. I still held the useless net, but I wasn't putting my hands into the water anywhere near that beast.

Noel stood there, up to his waist in water, equally unable to prevent the fish escaping. For once in his life, he was speechless, as the pike sailed out of the boathouse into the lough and away from us for ever.

We just watched it go, too stunned to speak.

And I never even caught a rudd that day.

A year or two later Noel caught a 30lb pike from this very spot, a pike not far short of the British Rod Caught Record at the time. Unfortunately I wasn't there to witness the capture, but I've always had a suspicion that it was our pike, the one we landed in the boat, the one who sailed away so happily, the one who had left us both speechless.

Big Jim

The only fisherman we ever met at Blessingbourne was Big Jim. Big Jim, as his name suggested, was a big man, well over six foot and muscular with it. When we were eleven Jim would probably be in his mid-twenties I suppose, a local man who lived in the cottages on the other side of the town lough.

Jim looked like a 1950s rock n roll star, Eddie Cochran or even Elvis Presley, with his black slicked-back hair and his black leather jacket with the zippers. He wore T shirts in the American fashion, to show off his bulging biceps I suspected. These handsome looks and his bulging biceps had, according to Noel, made Jim a very popular young man among the women of Fivemiletown. Or as Noel put it so eloquently, "Shure, he's ridden haff the town!"

I wasn't entirely sure what this meant, but took Noel's word for it.

Regardless of his exploits with the women of the town, Big Jim was a real fisherman through and through, being down there at the lough most nights, regardless of the weather conditions.

"Howzaboutyi boys!" he would greet us cheerily.

Jim was always friendly and always, it seemed, in a very good mood about something or other. I asked Noel about him one day, wondering about the cause of Jim's perpetual good humour.

"The wimmin can't keep thur hands off've him," Noel explained. "Jim's ridden that many winners he's thinking of entering the Grand National next year."

I said, "Is he a jockey then?" which caused Noel to almost wet himself with laughter.

"Oh aye, he's a jockey alright! Especially over the jumps!"

I didn't get what he was on about, but laughed anyway. It was sure to be something funny, as everything Noel said was funny, for he was a very comical character. I guessed his comment about Jim riding in the Grand National was actually something to do with girls, but as we had never seen him with a girl, I thought that this might have just been one of Noel's fanciful stories. He had a very vivid imagination, had Noel.

We usually met up with Big Jim on the lane by the gatehouse to the Blessingbourne estate, and would talk together with him towards the lough itself. Sometimes he would stay with us and fish by the boathouse, on the side of the lough by the big house. Often though, after an hour or two with us he would quietly take his leave and go off on his own to explore the far side of the lough.

We didn't join him there, as the far side of the lough was well-nigh unfishable for us boys. You needed to be tall enough to enable you to cast fifty yards or more over the lilypads and reeds into open water, and then even if you did somehow manage to hook a pike, it was impossible for youngsters to drag it over all these obstacles. Because of this handicap, Noel and I didn't go to the far side of the lough, being content to stay in the open water by the boathouse.

Another factor in keeping us on our bank was that the other side of the lough was dense woodland, mostly tall dark pine trees. Over the years these had created a soft carpet of pine needles underfoot, so that the ground was gentle and yielding, and the air was full of the pleasant scent of pine. This was the only attraction, because to me the pine woodland was dense and dark and somehow intimidating. I didn't like it at all.

The darkness and the air of secrecy was made worse by the thick laurel bushes which straddled the shore line. To reach the water you had to fight your way through these tough bushes. True, once you were at the water's edge there were secluded little bays among the laurels, open only to the lough, which were safe and secret places. In these bays you could sit unobserved and undisturbed, for no-one came here, only Big Jim.

After eating my tea at my uncle's house, I would meet up in the lane at the back of The Chestnut Bar with Noel. We fished so often that our rods were permanently tackled up and kept in the yard, ready to go. Noel would grin and show me the packet of fags or the little bottle of Captain Morgan he'd nicked from his dad's bar, and we'd get on our old bikes and wobble our way down the Main Street towards Blessingbourne, one hand on the handlebars, the other cradling the rods.

This particular night we met up with Jim as usual and fished together on our bank by the boathouse for an hour or so, then, without saying anything, Jim rose quietly and started packing his gear away.

Noel nudged me and winked. "Are yiz off then Jim?"

"I am boys."

"Round the other side?"

Jim nodded.

Noel was grinning and I could tell he was up to something, but of what it was, I had no idea.

We both watched as Jim made his way off through the bushes, and vanished from our sight. He was moving quickly, I noticed, as if intent on something purposeful.

Noel was watching his progress.

"What are you up to?" I asked Noel.

"Sssh!"

Noel put his finger to his lips. We waited in silence for a minute or two, listening to see that Jim was well on his way round the lough.

"I'll betcha he's riding tonight!"

"No, he's going fishing."

"Fishing be focked! The horny focker's seein a wumman." Noel got to his feet. "C'mon, let's go watch!"

I wasn't at all sure that this was a good idea, but it sounded exciting, so we put down our rods and carefully followed the path into the bushes that Big Jim had taken.

All the way round the lough we crept along, trying not to make any noise which might alert Jim that two young lads were on his trail, one lecherous and chuckling to himself, the other nervous about what might happen next.

As quietly as we could, we left the boggy wetland surrounding the lough and entered the pine forest. We sneaked along in silence, carefully watching where we were putting our feet down, anxious not to make a sound that might give us away. We were getting near now.

All of a sudden I began to panic. Jim might be courting with a girl and if we caught him at it, he might be very angry with us. I didn't want to spy on them anyway as I knew it would only lead to trouble, for Jim was a big man and he might have a big temper to match. I definitely didn't want to risk annoying him. I didn't want to go any further. Jim might be anywhere among the laurel bushes.

Suddenly Noel stopped. He sniffed the air, then grinned hugely. "Perfume! I told yi!"

This was very exciting I must admit, but also, I feared, very dangerous. Jim wasn't called Big Jim for nothing; he was indeed a big man and surely wouldn't take kindly to being spied on, especially if he was busy courting.

I pulled Noel's arm. "C'mon, leave him alone!"

"Fock aff!"

"Come on Noel, leave him be."

Noel was all for continuing on, but I was determined. As I'd plodded through the darkness after Noel, memories had come to me, nasty memories of Norma Greensit and what had gone on between us that day in O'Brien's shed.

I turned back. "Let's go!"

"Are you fockin scared?"

"Yes." I admitted it. "I'm fockin scared."

Noel stopped.

I shrugged. I was very uncomfortable about spying on Jim and his girlfriend.

Noel stood and looked at me for some time.

"Don't yiz want to watch?"

"No."

"Ach, chicken."

I didn't care that he called me names. I waited.

He could tell I was upset. He shrugged. "Oh, alright then. Let's go back." He grinned. "Chicken."

He was a good friend and he could tell I wanted to leave Jim and his girlfriend to their own pleasures. I turned back the way we had come and he followed me. Silently, we crept back to our side of the lough and resumed fishing.

For an hour or so we fished on, catching roach and perch, but saying very little. I knew that Noel loved a joke, and that he possessed a wicked sense of humour. All the time he was sitting there, watching his float, I could tell that his mind was working overtime at some scheme to catch Big Jim in the act of being a jockey.

Eventually he murmured, "I wonder what filly he's riding tonight."

He listened long and hard for a clue as to what was happening across the lough in the laurel bushes. Sounds usually travelled far across the still waters of the lough, but though he strained to hear, on this evening the wind was blowing from our shore towards the lovers, so nothing more was heard or seen from Jim and his secret woman, if indeed she existed at all.

The next night Jim was there again. As before, we met up with him at the gatehouse.

"Hiya boys!" he said brightly.

"Hiya Jim."

Noel nudged me. He had a mischievous grin on his face. "Are yiz fishin with us tonight Jim?"

"Aye. Maybe for an hour or two."

"Good fishin over thur is it?"

"It is." Jim wasn't going to give anything away.

Noel gave me a nudge with his elbow.

"Did youse catch much last night?"

"Just the wan."

He wasn't going to say any more, so we walked together into the estate in silence.

Noel nudged me again. He couldn't wait to hear details and was smiling to himself so much it was a wonder Big Jim hadn't noticed.

We tackled up and started fishing by the boathouse.

Noel was the first to speak. "What're you after catching tonight Jim?"

By now Noel was grinning and barely able to control his laughter.

Jim just stood there, staring at the pike bung and the livebait he'd cast out in the lough. He said nothing.

We fished together for an hour, before Jim started glancing at his watch.

Noel elbowed me to pay attention. "Are yiz expectin someone Jim?"

"No, no boys. Just keeping an eye on the time."

At seven o' clock he reeled in and sighed. "Nothin much doin here boys. Think I might try over the other side."

Noel winked at me. "Thur's nothing doing here. We might as well come with yiz."

Jim started. "Ah no lads, I like to be on me own sometimes. Get away from it all. Peace and quiet y'know."

"Ah come on now Jim, we'll come with yiz. Keep ye company." Noel reeled in as if to leave and follow him.

Jim had already packed up his rod and was clearly anxious to be on his way.

Noel stood beside him. "Are ye sure ye don't want some company Jim?"

"NO!" the poor man blurted and with that he disappeared hotfoot into the undergrowth.

When he was well out of sight Noel burst out laughing.

"He's off over the gallops."

"What?"

"He's off ridin the wumman again!"

I wished he'd forget about Jim and whatever was going on. I just wanted to fish for pike and not think about what might be happening over there in the darkness of the laurel bushes.

But this time we did hear them, for Jim had forgotten that sounds travel far across water, especially water as still and quiet as the lough was that night. There was no wind and every sound was magnified. We sat there, not saying a word, me embarrassed and not knowing what was going on, Noel clearly dying to hear what was going to happen.

First there was Jim, a low, deep note, then a light voice, a woman's voice. There was some conversation, then the conversation stopped.

We couldn't make out the words being said and so could only imagine what was going on, then the sounds returned, much louder now. Only this time she wasn't saying much in the way of words.

"Oh," came the woman's voice. "Oh Jim!"

She sounded pleased about something.

I glanced at Noel, my face reddening. Noel raised two thumbs and grinned lecherously.

Then the sounds came more urgently.

"Oh… oh…"

And more insistently.

"Oh… Oh… Oh…"

And then, "Oh Jim!"

The sounds were getting much louder and more frequent. Whatever Jim was saying to her she must have enjoyed it, judging by the excited note of pleasure in her voice.

The couple obviously had no idea that every sound was echoing round the lough, or that Noel was sitting there enthralled by the entertainment.

I glanced at Noel. He was enjoying every moment, thumping his thighs in delight.

From across the lough the sounds grew louder and more insistent. She was calling out now, the sounds getting faster.

"Oooh! Oooh! Oooh!" she gasped.

"Oooh! Oooh! Oooh!" mimicked Noel to me.

I kicked out at him. "Ssssh! They'll hear!"

"Fock aff! This is great crack!"

Then from the other shore came a shout, and a shriek. "Oooh Jim!"

I was embarrassed and glanced unhappily at Noel. He wasn't embarrassed, he was busting a gut laughing.

Then came a final, "OOOH OOOH OOOH!" and a great big sigh, before the sounds subsided into silence.

I was bright red, my ears burning with shame. I didn't know what to say or do.

Noel did though, he burst out clapping! As fiercely as he could, he slapped his hands together, all the time laughing and jumping about. The loud claps rolled across the water.

"Good on yiz!" Noel called out, as loudly as he could.

The sound spilled across the lough.

I was aghast. "What did you do that for?"

"Fun!" he laughed, then cupping his hands to his

mouth, he called, "Give her another wan Jim! We enjoyed that!"

Across the lough I could hear voices, an angry woman's voice, Jim's lower voice. Then there were more angry words, followed by the noise of someone running through the woods, brushing aside the bushes and the undergrowth in haste.

"C'mon!" I said, panicking. "Let's get out of here. He'll kill us!"

We grabbed our rods and tackle and ran for home.

We didn't see or hear from Big Jim for a week. His visits to the lough with his young lady were no more.

Then one night, eight days later, he was there at the gatehouse waiting for us. I didn't know what to expect from him, and was apprehensive.

Not Noel though. "Hiya Jim!" he greeted brightly.

"Hiya boys! Howzabout yi?"

I relaxed a little, as Big Jim seemed perfectly at ease. Maybe he hadn't guessed that it was us two who were the phantom clappers of Blessingbourne lough. Maybe he wasn't angry with us, who could tell? He was a very cool customer.

"Fishin with us tonight Jim?"

"I am boys, if that's fine with you."

Nothing more was said, and we baited our rods and stood in the reeds by the boathouse and fished together for an hour or more. Then seven o' clock came.

Noel jabbed me with his landing net to alert me to the fun. "Are yiz staying with us tonight Jim?"

"I am boys."

"Not trying the other side?"

"No. I think I'll stay here."

There was silence. Noel was grinning.

Jim turned to us both; he was grinning too.

"It was you, you young fockers, wasn't it?"

I didn't know what he was going to do next, but I needn't have worried, for instead of hitting us he burst out laughing.

"I'm tellin ye boys, when she heard yiz clappin she pulled up her knickers and ran like a fockin rabbit!"

We all stood there in the water, roaring our heads off at the thought, me included. I wasn't entirely sure what I was laughing about, but it was very funny.

It was fully ten minutes before we started to fish again.

Jim was standing there in the reeds threading a new roach onto the hooks. Then he glanced at us, both still chuckling to ourselves, and that set him off laughing once again.

"Ah well," he said philosophically. "Shure, she was getting too clingy for my liking! I'm best rid."

He swung his rod back, ready to cast.

"And anyway," he added with a smile, "There's plenty more fish in the lough!"

"Aye," said Noel. "Pussy fish!"

They both roared at that. I had never heard of a fish called a pussy fish, but I laughed along with them.

The Bomb

It was later that same summer, when Noel made the bomb.

The summer had been long and hot. The land was parched, for it hadn't rained in Ireland since March. The sun shone every day and all day. Nothing like it had been heard of in Ireland, where it rains at least briefly on most days of the year.

Old men in The Chestnut Bar scratched their heads, then their groins.

"A drap of porter there Tommy!"

Thus fortified, they wiped the white froth from their moustaches and exclaimed, "It's the fockin Russians!"

The cows on my uncle's farm developed dehydration illnesses and had to have special magic potions to help them recover.

The grass turned brown.

The bogs and the river dried out and soon there wasn't a trout to be had. With such low, clear conditions it was impossible to catch a fish, for they were hidden under the banks of the rivers in their safe holes, before you could get a fly cast anywhere near them. Nor would they look at worms.

I was sitting with Noel, son of Tommy Mills, the publican of The Chestnut Bar. We were on empty crates in his back yard, grumbling about the weather.

"It's fockin desprit," sighed Noel, looking up at yet another cloudless sky.

The back lane was full of wrecked cars from my uncle's garage, simmering in the heat. He was always short of space to store them, and for years he had been filling the back lane with shattered wrecks, intending one day to repair or restore them. He was taking his time getting round to the restoration jobs. Some of the wrecks had been there over twenty years and now had quite tall trees growing out of bonnets and windows.

Noel and I clambered over the wreckage of battered Fords, ancient Austins and mangled Morrises, looking for something interesting to steal. The air smelled of old leather and hot painted metal. Some of the oldest cars had leather seats, now sprouting cancerous horsehair growths, for mice had got inside and made nests in the stuffing. We enjoyed a short but unsuccessful Mouse Hunt.

For some reason by this time in the summer we had tired of fishing the loughs, and were only interested in trout – in search of which we roamed the countryside for miles around, on two old bikes which belonged in the back lane. No-one ever laid claim to them, and they were used by whoever took a fancy to riding them, though they were always returned intact.

Adults never bothered us – Noel's dad had the Bar to run, my uncle worked twenty-four hours a day running the garage, his car showroom, several farms and a horse-breeding business. My aunt seemed to run a nonstop cafe feeding a tribe of mechanics, farm workers and a whole host of kids she was 'looking after' for someone. We were on our own.

"Let's go down to Cooneen river," I suggested.

Noel curled his lip in disdain. "Ah, what's the fockin point? Shure, the river's drained away entirely. Thur'd be more watter in it if youse had a pish!"

He was right. The last time we'd tried our favourite place we hadn't seen a fish all day.

"Shure," he added, spitting emphatically. "We cuddent catch a fish thur if we wuz to net the hoors!"

He stopped. A bright idea had occurred to him. Then, just as quickly as it had appeared, it vanished. It was the heat.

"Ach, what's the use? We haven't got the use of an oul net anyway."

There was a clacking of heavy hooves and some black and white cows came round the corner, followed by my cousin Kenneth and his dog Wee Tiny.

I waved a desultory hand. I didn't like cows, I didn't like doing nothing. If only it wasn't so bright and sunny, if only it would rain……

"What we need is a good thunderstorm Noel."

Noel brightened. "Ah by God, we'll catch the hoors then! They'll be out uv them oul holes then beGod!"

Then he looked up at the cloudless sky and the glitter went from his eyes. He hacked at a stone embedded in the lane.

"Ach, if ony it'd rain!"

For weeks we tried and tried again. We cycled miles. We used every trick we knew. We worm fished, we fly fished. We used bloodworms. All we could catch were salmon parr – poor brainless parodies of trout which would take anything cast to them.

"Jesus, this is fockin ridiculous!" Noel shouted bitterly, as we cycled home after yet another hopeless day. "If it doesn't rain soon I'll be goin over the Watter to catch fish!"

'Over the Watter' meant England. We both laughed at the absurdity of such a suggestion.

Then Noel stopped laughing. A bright idea had occurred to him and he couldn't do two things at once –

ride a bike and think up bright ideas at the same time – so he stopped.

"It's a fockin brainwave!" he roared. "I'm a fockin genius!"

"What is it?"

He gripped my arm excitedly. "Have y'ivver heard of carbide bombs?"

I confessed I hadn't.

"They're explosive! We could make one and blow the fockers out!"

I liked the sound of this.

"It's what they used to do in the oul days."

Now this sounded like fun. At home I was interested in chemistry, especially the explosive possibilities of certain chemical reactions. In our garden shed I had a whole stock of dangerous chemicals given to me by my dad's brother, Uncle George, who worked as a scientist in a laboratory. As a result of his naïve and trusting generosity I had dangerous elements and compounds no teenage boy should be let loose with, especially a boy as obsessed with munitions as I was. I often packed tins with weed killer, magnesium strip and iron filings to make home-made bombs. I liked explosions.

"Where'll we get this carbide stuff though?"

Noel grinned. "Tommy Carruth," he said with confidence. "He sells it for batteries."

The following day found us again in the back lane among the wrecked cars. This time we were armed with a very large tin of Calcium Carbide and some smaller tins, in which to pack the stuff to make an explosive device. We were going to blow the fish out of their holes under the banks. It was indeed a brilliant idea, but one we thought best to keep to ourselves.

I must confess also that I was beginning to have one or two reservations, like how much of the stuff we'd bought. From my explosions at home I knew that it didn't take much weed-killer to make a very big bang. If carbide was as explosive as weed-killer, we'd blow up half the town. The very large tin of carbide we'd got from Carruth's shop would make about a dozen bombs.

"What I can't understand Noel, is – how's it going to explode?"

Noel seemed a man possessed, working away, digging the stuff out of the big tin with a spoon.

"Noel. Stop a minute. What makes it go off?"

He stopped digging. "Fockin Englishman! Have yiz no faith in me?"

"Course I have Noel, it's just… how do we make it explode?"

"It explodes on contact with watter, ye eejit!"

"Oh."

Thus assured, I continued scooping handfuls of the stuff into the large empty paint tin we had appropriated from my uncle's garage, to use as our bomb container. I knew from my experiments at home that explosives worked best when compressed into a small space.

Soon it was finished. I rammed the lid on tight and banged it shut with a rock.

"Right then Noel, what are we going to use for a fuse?"

"A fuse?" Noel looked blank. "What the fock's a fuse?"

I was beginning to have even more reservations about Noel's skills as a bomb-making carbide fisherman.

"It's a timing device. Something that allows you to get to safety before the whole bloody thing goes up in your face."

I spoke from some experience, having almost killed myself several times with explosions at home.

Noel however, flush with the enthusiasm of his new idea, dismissed my fears as groundless. Before we set off on our first bombing run, we wrapped the paint tin into an old coat we'd found, to disguise its proper purpose. Having packed the gallon paint tin tight full of carbide I had a fair idea of its explosive potential.

And off we went on our bikes. Yelling and laughing, we sailed off down the Spout Lane to the deepest fishing hole we knew, under the bridge at Pulboys Cross.

Here was an old stone bridge, crossing the little river at a point where it formed a decent-sized and quite deep pool. We parked our bikes and went to look down over the parapet. There were big trout down there somewhere in holes under the bridge and it was our intention to set off the bomb, stun the fish, and then net the whole lot of them for ourselves.

In the absence of any fusing mechanism, there followed a short discussion of who was to actually throw the bomb into the water. It went something like this.

"Go on then Noel, chuck it in!"

"Fock aff! You throw it!"

"It was your idea!"

"Yes but I'm too fockin young to die."

It wasn't that we were scared – we were excited, but we had no idea what the effects of the bomb might be. It might not explode, it might blow up the bridge… so no, we weren't scared. We were consumed by images of a pile of stunned trout floating on the surface of the pool, and the fear of the unknown was an added bonus.

At least it was to me. Noel didn't give a 'fock.'

Noel was quite sure that he was a fockin genius and as he was the inventor who had done all the brainwork, I should be the one to set it off and have the honour of actually launching the bomb into the water below the bridge.

I had uncomfortable memories of the destructive powers of packed explosive. I had once detonated a small tin of Sodium Chlorate, Iron Filings, Sulphur and some secret ingredients in our back garden, using a strip of magnesium ribbon as a fuse. I had then hidden behind the wall separating us from our neighbours.

The resulting shattering explosion had blown the windows out of our garden shed, frightened Mrs Next Door into an Hysterical Fit (she claimed she was on the toilet at the time and would never recover) – and caused three of our guinea pigs to run away from home, never to be seen again.

I knew what bombs could do, so I gave it to Noel, who didn't.

Secretly I doubted if this bomb of Noel's would work, but in our present desperately fishless condition anything was worth trying. My misgivings about the ethics of our enterprise were forgotten in the thrill of it all.

Noel was too fat to run fast, so he crouched low down behind the stone parapet of the bridge and watched as I lobbed the bomb over the wall into the pool below.

We put fingers in our ears. We waited.

All we heard was a solid, thunking splash, a few gurgling bubbles, then silence.

"Some fockin bomb that!" grumbled Noel.

"Wait."

We covered our ears with our hands, closed our eyes, and crouched waiting for the bang. After all, carbide exploded on contact with water, it just needed time to get wet. We'd punched little holes in the lid and surely……

There was no explosion. We waited and waited. I opened one eye, removed one hand, nudged Noel to stand up and look over the parapet.

"Fockin thing's sunk without trace," he announced in disgust.

I came out from behind the stone wall and joined him looking down into the pool.

"It might be just taking its time," I suggested hopefully.

We stood there, leaning over, looking down at the depths, afraid to move in case it did go off, afraid to leave it in case we missed something exciting like a river suddenly full of stunned trout.

Neither of us noticed the priest approaching.

"Hello there boys, how's about ye?" (This was the local greeting.)

I nearly fell over the wall with the shock.

Noel turned to face the priest, his face a picture of horror.

"Ah, hello there father," he managed to say.

The priest wasn't a young man. In fact he was a very old, very frail, white-haired old man. He wheezed musically as he dismounted his bike, pushing his equally ancient machine over to the bridge. He was coming to join us!

I grabbed Noel's arm in a panic and hissed, "What are

we going to do?"

The old priest, innocent of our fears, hoisted himself onto the low stone parapet and sat down next to us.

'Oh my God,' I thought. Little did he know what was down there!

"Any luck with the fishing boys? Shure isn't it a desprit drought this year."

I noticed then that he had a fishing rod strapped to his bike. My God, what if he started fishing here? What if the bomb went off and killed the priest? We'd be crucified for murdering a man of God!

Noel slid off the wall suddenly, as if his mind was made up. Seizing his bike he gabbled, "Nice seeing you father," and made to move off.

"Och, you're not away already are yiz? Always in a rush the young today…"

"Yes father, me da's got jobs for me to do."

The old priest smiled benevolently. "Ah that does me good to hear it. You help your daddy then do you?"

"Yes father."

"Ah now I come to think of it, you're Tommy Mills' boy, aren't ye?"

Noel's eyes rolled uncomfortably round his head.

We were both thinking, 'what if the bloody bomb goes off?'

Then the priest turned to me. "And what about your young friend here? He doesn't have much to say for himself now, does he?"

"No father. He's from across the water."

"Ah, poor soul. I don't suppose he's ever seen a fish worth the name."

"No father."

Noel was kicking me furiously, trying to get us moving away. "Come on now David," he hissed to me. "You know what your aunt said about getting back early."

"She did?"

"She did shurely!"

It dawned on me that he meant to abandon the poor old priest to whatever might be happening in the pool below.

Meanwhile the priest was uncoupling the rod from his bike, obviously intending to fish the pool where the bomb lay simmering beneath us. I hoped for some heavenly intervention, some help from above for one of his own.

By now Noel had abandoned all pretence of politeness, and was already mounted on his bike, heading for home.

I climbed slowly onto my old boneshaker and started off after him.

"Noel!" I called. Just as the bomb went off.

We were no more than ten yards from the bridge. There was an unnatural GER-RUMPH! from the river, and a fountain of water shot up in the air. The poor old priest leapt for cover, moving faster than he'd done in forty years…

"Noel!" I called, but too late. He was tearing up that lane, his fat bum pumping the pedals as if the Devil himself was after him.

Which in a way, I suppose, he was.

Aughentaine

By late August of that scorching summer the Northern Ireland government made an official proclamation just in case people hadn't noticed - there really was a drought. Hosepipes were banned. The fields were brown. Cows lay about all day panting, too tired to stand. Dogs slept in the dust by the cattle mart.

Kids went swimming every day to the town lough, which had warmed to unheard-of temperatures. Somewhere in Ireland the shrivelled body of a man was found in a dried-up bog, revealed for the first time in thousands of years. He had been murdered.

Noel and I hadn't caught a fish in weeks. Instead of enjoying ourselves out in the country, we lounged around in town, waiting on street corners for something to happen, or getting in the way of the mechanics in my uncle's garage.

"Can't yiz go fishin?" they'd ask in irritation.

We shook our heads and still got in their way.

Noel took to lifting fags from behind his dad's bar counter, and we took them to the swimming lough, where they attracted the interest of several girls, and got us into a fight with a tough lad called Willy Watson. We decided we would stick to fishing.

At teatime at Uncle Jack's we all sat down to eat together. There were so many to feed we had to have two sittings at the table - I was on the first sitting with Paddy and Billy Beattie from the garage, my cousins Eric and Kenneth, my brother and two little boys my aunt kept an eye on while their mother was out at work.

It was another hot day and all the windows were open. The room was stifling, because it had a corrugated iron roof and my aunt had been cooking food all day. The dogs were lying around the room looking sorry for themselves. Then my Aunt Martha brought in the big dish full of baked spuds for us all – I loved them all split and flaky and steaming. I could eat Irish spuds as a meal on their own.

Paddy was talking about the stock car they'd been making in their spare time at the garage. Aunt Martha came up from the kitchen with plates full of stew. "There, that should keep yiz all quiet for an hour or two."

And then suddenly it began. Big heavy raindrops thudded onto the roof, just one or two at first, then pattering together into a drumbeat.

We all stopped what we were doing to listen.

"Good job yiz got the hay in Missiz Gray," Paddy said.

I was at the window, looking out into the yard. The sunburned roofs of the wrecked cars in the garden were covered with dark blotches.

"Sounds like rain!" I exclaimed.

"Shut the winder then eejit!" said Aunt Martha. I sat down, for she had a hefty slap on her.

"It's actually raining!"

"That boy'll go far," said someone.

"I wish he would," said my brother. "Then I could have his spuds."

I was too excited to reply. The rain was speeding up in tempo. This was no light flurry, but a real thunderstorm. Soon the rivers would fill and the fish would be out feeding in a frenzy after all the drought.

"Will ye sit down and eat the food I cooked for yiz!"

Reluctantly, I obeyed, pulling a baked spud out of the pile. Then the outside door banged open and there stood Noel, panting, wild-eyed, fishing rod in hand.

"Are yiz coming?"

I jumped up.

"Coming where?" said Aunt Martha.

"Fishin Missiz Gray. The rain's come, the river's floodin!"

"After he's eaten!"

"But Missiz!"

"No buts. I'm not having his mother sayin I starved the cuddy!" (a cuddy is a boy)

Noel hopped round with impatience. "I'll get the wurrums!" he shouted, running off down the passage. "See yiz outside in five minits!"

Two minutes later, my mouth full of scalding baked spud, I was out in the back lane. The rain was belting down now, kicking up the dust into clouds. Already the air felt fresher. Blue and grey clouds were filling the sky. It looked wonderful.

Noel hurtled round the corner, hugging the grips of his bike. Two tin cans dangled from the handlebars.

"Ready?"

"Let's go!"

I picked up the other old bike. We didn't care that the evening light was fading early, or that menacing blue thunderclouds were building up over the Sperrin Mountains away to the west. It was raining! It was great!

"Where're we off to?" I shouted as we tore up the wet Main Street.

"Aughentaine."

I'd never heard of it, but trusted to his judgement. There was nothing the Mills family didn't know about fishing.

Some of the old fellers who usually sat outside the Valley Hotel were sheltering in doorways. They waved and laughed at us as we stood on the pedals to get more speed.

"Hey boys!" they called. "Bring us back a fush!"

Once up the Main Street, the village ended and we were out on the open road to Clogher. Without waterproofs we were already soaked to the skin, but it was a warm night and we were hot from riding and anyway, as Noel shouted, "Shure, the watter's nice and wet!"

"Slow down," I called. "What's the rush?"

"They'll all be out tonight, you'll see."

I wondered what he meant.

We turned off the main road and down a steeply-winding lane, riding between high green hedges. It was nearly dark because of the storm and we had no lights. Then suddenly Noel slid off his bike and dumped it, wheels still spinning, into a ditch. We were next to a lichen-covered stone bridge.

I followed Noel and ran to see the water beneath. There was a tiny stream, but it was rapidly filling up, boiling brown, rising as we watched. Soon it was roaring round the bridge supports and surging up the banks. What had just a few moments ago been a placid trickle was now a treacly torrent.

We tackled up quickly, using thick pike lines, big hooks and the large worms for salmon fishing, which Noel had stolen from his dad. Then we were off, hurrying downstream, peering at the banks, looking for eddies.

It was useless trying to throw the worm into the main stream, as it would simply be swept away and would never reach the bottom. I was excited, reminded of the days back home, when I used to fish the little Crimple Beck with bullheads under the banks, looking for trout in hidden holes.

It was dark now and we were stumbling over tall tussocks and bogland.

"Ah shit!" howled Noel, as he fell and went in up to his hips in thick black bog. He struggled out, bog juice up to his waist.

Twenty yards downstream we found what we were looking for – at the end of a straight stretch the stream curved and cut under a bank on the opposite shore. On our side was a cattle wallow – a dark muddy bank of flooded hoof prints. Normally it would be shallow and fishless, but now it was an eddy - the perfect spot for fish sheltering from the fury of the flood.

We both cast in. The single lead shot on mine was sufficient to take the big worm down in the relatively calm water. It drifted round in the undercurrents, but stayed safely out of the raging flood. Here – hopefully – trout would be lying, seeking protection, foraging for the food the flood had brought them.

The line jagged instantly. A bite! Another sharp jag. I released the line from my hand and held it loose so the fish wouldn't feel any fisherman's weight on the other end.

BANG!

The fish took the worm and ran. I tightened the line, snapped the bar over and he was on.

There was no time for skill, no time for ceremony. I pulled hard and swung him straight out, wriggling and twisting and no doubt startled, up onto the bank. There I fell on him, using both hands – for it was a belter of a fish, a couple of pounds of wild Irish trout. A fish like this was unbelievable after the long fishless weeks of the summer we'd had.

"Will you just look at that!" I shouted, proud, shaking with excitement.

For a second we both stood still in the dark and stared at it. Then I banged it on the head and ran for another worm.

In a moment Noel had one too, and soon we were into more. Tugging, fighting, losing some – it was insane – the fish were taking every cast. Sometimes in our panic and excitement we struck too soon, but we didn't care, the fish were going mad and so were we.

We fell over, we fell in, we caught fish, we lost fish.

"Hey fockin Englishman! How's this for fishin?"

"It's bloody great!" I shouted. "I've got another!"

"Me too!" he yelled, pulling at this rod. "If anywun sees us, they'll think we're from Purdysburn!" (The Northern Ireland Mental Institution.)

There was no sense of time. We might have been there an hour, it might have been four. It was pitch black now. We were covered in mud and rain and bog juice and trout. We'd fallen in half a dozen times – but we were oblivious to the mess we were in.

Between us we'd got a dozen or more, laid out in rows on the bank. Noel's and mine, long silver bars of trout – and what trout! For weeks we'd fished these streams without the sign of anything bigger than a six-inch salmon parr, and now we had a bankful of beasties.

"I don't believe it!" I panted. "We're dreaming this!"

Noel, crouched over, unhooking another fish, leapt up roaring madly, dancing about and cackling like a maniac, his arms full of the fish he'd caught.

Suddenly, I realised we were not alone. Out of the wet blackness stumbled two figures. Big, black-haired men in coats tied with garden twine, dark bearded faces half-covered by tattered old hats. Fishermen? What could they be?

We stopped shouting, guilty and surprised and not a little scared. We stood still, staring at them. They had saplings in their hands, not rods. They had pulled the twigs off these and at the end had attached bits of thick string, the sort used to tie hay bales. They had no reels, just a foot of nylon line at the end of the string. To us they looked like creatures from another world, belted up in their old brown coats with soggy hats over their faces. Neither of them spoke.

Then they saw our fish and because they were fishermen we had no fear of them. They grinned big bad-toothed smiles and squatted down beside us to show us their catches.

Their overcoat pockets were stuffed with fish – one of them the size of a grilse (a summer salmon) the rest over two pounds each – and all of them caught on a bit of baling string and a branch!

Noel laid his fish out. I lifted mine from under their covers of wet docken leaves. The wild men whistled appreciatively and nudged each other. Noel and I grinned proudly.

Then without a word the wild men rose and squelched off into the dark from where they'd come.

"Mountain men," said Noel.

We stopped eventually, exhausted by the excitement. The fish were still feeding, but we simply couldn't carry any more home. We had no creels or bags or anything. I jammed the pockets of my sodden parka full; the other trout we threaded with line through mouth and gills and dangled them from the handlebars of our bikes.

As we rode back, the fish were heavy and wet and slapped against our bare legs, but who cared? We biked through the dark without lights and without a care in the world, drunk on our feast of fish, singing our favourite song, 'Walking Back To Happiness!' as loudly as we could, all the way home.

We dumped the bikes in the back lane.

"See yiz in the morning," said Noel. He nudged me and grinned. "Fockin great, wasn't it?"

I grinned too. "It fockin was!"

Noel went off down the lane to the pub. I stumbled towards the back yard.

I was suddenly aware that it was no longer quite as dark as it had been. I put my hand through the hole in the corrugated iron fence of my uncle's back yard, and drew the bolt open. The gate creaked. A light went on upstairs.

"Who the fock's that?" came Uncle Jack's voice.

"It's me."

"Who the fock's me?"

Uncle Jack appeared at the top of the stairs, poker in hand. Aunt Martha joined him, hair in curlers, rolling pin in hand.

"Thank God you're back!" she said, "Ye had us worried half to death y'boy yi!"

Guiltily I shut the gate behind me and climbed wearily up the steps over the stables. I was exhausted, the heavy fish weighing me down.

The family were all up now, uncle and aunt, cousins and my brother Eck.

Aunt Martha grabbed hold of me. "Whur've ye been til this time, ye young cub?"

"Fishing!" I said proudly, spilling fish out of my pockets for them all to see.

I think they must have realised it was pointless telling me off, even though it was now daylight. I was too full of fabulous fishing to listen to anything they had to say.

Inside the kitchen, they gathered round as I pulled fish after fish out of my pockets, one by one. The trout were wet, slippery, and some of them bent out of shape, but they were all great trout.

Even Uncle Jack, who was no fisherman, was impressed enough to say, "Jazus, that's some quare fush ye've got thur!"

We laid them out in rows on the draining board, and stared big-eyed.

Jack tousled my hair. "You're some fisherman wee lad!"

"We'll feed haff the town," said Martha.

Later, when they had dragged me away from my fish and up to bed, I lay awake in the dawn light, too thrilled to sleep, still fighting fish in my mind.

I suppose nowadays I would have put all or most of them back, but I was eleven years old and carried away by the magic of it all. The darkness, the sudden flood, the excitement of catching fish after the long drought, the wild men of the mountains with their sticks and bits of string –

and the trout themselves, the great golden fish with spotted flanks of silver, black and red, that we'd found so unexpectedly. What fishing eh? Never the like of it before or since.

There would never be another day like it, for Aughtentaine is in East Tyrone and a few short years later the Troubles began. No English man or boy would be safe there until the next century.

I have never been back. I want my memory of that wonderful night to stay with me for ever. I know in my heart that the changes that will have taken place won't be for the better, so for me Aughentaine stays as it was, not as it might be today. Two boys careering on old bikes down a lane in the dark. They are wet and dirty and tired, but they don't care. They yell their happiness into the night air, for dangling from their handlebars are trout, huge wild trout hauled out of a tiny stream.

No, the only time I'll ever ride a bike home from Aughentaine will be in my dreams.

Part Two

Would it not be delightful in these leaden times, if we might carry our friends along with us, back to those golden days?

Romilly Fedden

Pud's Pike

This salutary tale illustrates the fate that awaits all those foolish enough to boast – whether it be boasting of their fishing prowess, their fishing tackle, or their fishing opportunities. With me in this instance it was the last of these three weaknesses. I was thirteen at the time and that summer I learned a sharp lesson in life, one which I've never forgotten, and which I will now tell you about.

Two years earlier I had passed my 11+ and had won a scholarship to a very minor public school. I was to be a Day Boy, not a Boarder, as the school was only a couple of bus journeys away from our home. I was pleased to have passed – not as pleased as my parents, who were delighted – but on the whole I was looking forward to my new school.

There I soon had a great friend, another scholarship boy, another Day Boy, called Martin. That was his official name, but it was only ever used by his mother. Everyone else called him Pud. This was because there was a character in a comic of the time, a youth about our own age, who was always having schemes and plans which invariably turned out badly. This youth was called Dimworthy, and according to those who knew me, this youth had an uncanny resemblance to yours truly.

Dimworthy had a dog, a faithful hound, which was his constant companion, and who inevitably suffered mishaps engineered by the scatter-brained and foolish Dimworthy.

Can you see where this one is going?

The hound was called Pud.

The real-life Pud was intensely loyal, a great friend and my constant companion, so much so that he was rather proud of the nickname, and accepted its use with his usual cheerful grin.

Pud, like me, was only at the school because they awarded a handful of scholarships out to local kids and Pud too had won one of these, by virtue of his considerable intelligence. Scholarship boys were Day Boys in a school which was over 90% fee-paying Boarders. We soon discovered that this was not a happy mix.

We were hated by the Boarders because of our freedom, (we went home at 4.00, the Boarders were incarcerated in the school for the entire term.) Day Boys were victimized because they had won scholarships and were therefore Swots, Pubes or Plebs, and as the average Boarder had an IQ marginally above that of a root vegetable, they resented anyone able to read and write.

The Boarders mostly came from well-off West Riding families, who were able to pay the ridiculously-expensive fees each term, whereas the Scholarship-winning Day Boys often came from relatively impoverished backgrounds, having won their places because of their brains, not the size of their father's wallets. The Boarders resented the fact that Day Boys had their fees paid by the local authority, so this was not a recipe for a happy school.

There were other problems for the Day Boys. The Boarders had all been together for four years, having started at age seven in the school Prep department. They resented the arrival of these swotty newcomers. Worse still, for some unknown reason, the school authorities had decided that Day Boys should skip a year, so when we started at age eleven we were placed in class 2A, meaning that we were at least a year younger than the Boarders in our class. Often the gap was as much as two years, because pupils who failed to pass the Promotion Exams each summer were held back a year. Invariably, as a large number of the Boarders were descended from Cro Magnon

Man and were thus barely able to read, they were held back. So it was that the Day Boys, most of whom were little boys wearing their first pair of long trousers, were in classes dominated by much older, much bigger, and much hairier boys.

Add to this unhappy mix the fact that Martin Bradley, aka Fartin Madly, aka Pud, was very short-sighted, his bottle glasses being a constant source of amusement to the dim-witted thugs of the school, thugs who liked to remove his glasses and torment him as he stumbled blindly about the room. It was so enjoyable it became a daily ritual.

I tried to stick up for him, but thanks to the administrative incompetence of the school authorities, instead of Pud being in 2A and later 3A with me and the other eight scholarship boys, Pud had been placed a C form. This class was full of retards who had been kept down year after year owing to their total inability to pass anything in the way of exams, thirty moronic louts interested only in Rugby and Masturbation. With these charming young men Pud had a hard time. Nevertheless, he was a cheery soul and never complained, being always good-natured and kind-hearted.

I spent many happy days at the house of the Pud family. His mother, known to us both as Ma Pud, was a generous and open-minded woman, who tolerated the often-idiotic teenage schemes dreamed up by Dimworthy and followed by his faithful hound Pud, in a way that never seemed possible at our house. My mother would have gone mad at some of the tricks we got up to, but not Ma Pud. She would always smile at our foolishness and often rescue us from whatever scrapes Dimworthy had got the pair of boys into, like the Great Horse Race Betting Scandal.

Now it so happened that barely half a mile from Pud's house was the Stonefall Brickworks, which over the years had produced many of the bricks which built our town. Recently however, it had fallen on hard times and had closed down. The site had been abandoned and the buildings demolished. The Brickworks pond, which once had been managed and maintained by judicious pumping, had then rapidly enlarged and filled with water. After a year it was well on its way to becoming a fair-sized lake. And it was in this condition that we discovered it.

Ever in search of cheap fishing (or preferably, completely free fishing) we delighted in the appearance of this nearby amenity and spent many happy hours on its bank, fishing away until darkness sent us home.

The Brickworks pond didn't have any large fish, but it quickly filled with a lot of small perch and silvery roach, so that it was good fun fishing for two boys with no money to spend on the membership of proper angling clubs. There was always the possibility, however unlikely, that somewhere out there in those deep and rapidly-filling waters, there might lurk a big fish, a pike.

Pud's grandad had given him for his birthday present a huge pike lure – a great red and silver spoon, called a Colorado. It had red wool wrapped round its large treble hooks, and Pud spent many hours hurling this great lure across the Brickworks pond waters, much to my amusement.

He caught nothing of course. There were no huge pike in the pond, how could there be – until the previous year it had only been a tiny pond thirty yards across. Pud however, was not to be deterred, for among his many qualities, was a steely determination. It was this that saw him through the endless days of bullying by the onanistic rugby thugs of 3C.

I can't remember what I was like at thirteen. No longer a boy, not yet looking at the girls. Time has a way of mellowing things and altering perspectives. In my own fond imagination I was a quiet, studious boy, interested in history and politics, one who fancied himself as an intellectual, one with a secret sympathy for the underdog, perhaps even a secret rebel. In sporting terms, I was a frustrated cricket star, as yet undiscovered by the myopic cricket staff of my school, and hence languishing with the incompetent dolts of the Eighth Side Game, boys who could barely tell one end of a cricket bat from the other, let alone use one to effect.

However, it seems that I was not averse to the odd boast, and the only thing I could possibly boast about was my link to the prestigious fishing club known as Knaresborough Anglers. My Grandad George Henry had been an early member, some time around 1900. A lifelong and skilful fisherman, he had passed his membership onto his son George, my dad's twin brother.

The exclusive Knaresborough Anglers owned some of the best trout waters for miles around, a great long stretch of the River Nidd, all the way from Hampsthwaite village down to Killinghall bridge, and recently Uncle George had started to take me along with him. His own children, two boys and two girls, were not interested in fishing and so it was that early on a Sunday morning, Uncle George would arrive at our house, collect me, and take me fishing with him to the Nidd.

Unfortunately, it seems that I had taken to referring to this treat constantly, and to the large number of trout I was able to catch there. (The trout were stock fish from a trout farm, and were, in truth, quite easy to catch.)

Each week I would regale Pud with tales of my fishing prowess, even in the presence of his mother. She, highly tolerant though she was, must have begun to tire of my boasting, for their family were not wealthy, and Pud would never be able to afford membership of such an exclusive and expensive fishing club as Knaresborough Anglers.

It must have irritated her to hear me constantly telling poor Pud how many trout I had caught and how easy they were to catch. All Pud had to look forward to was casting his Grandad's huge red Colorado spoon across the Brickworks pond in the forlorn hope that a pike might somehow be seduced by its colourful charms.

I was blissfully ignorant of any offence I might be causing, mainly because thirteen-year-old boys are almost always blissfully ignorant about most things, but also because good-natured old Pud would never have taken offence, he was so easy-going.

As the summer term of that year drew on, and the holidays neared, it became time in our family to think about going to Ireland, as we did every year. In those peaceful days we spent every summer with our relatives: Uncle Jack and our cousins in Co Tyrone, Aunt Peggy and our cousins in Co Cavan, or Grandad Johnny and the hundred perch in Co Monaghan.

The prospect of such thrilling fishing always excited me, and unfortunately began to lead me into even more boasting to Pud. Ireland was real fishing, I always asserted. The fishing was free, the fish were abundant, and they were everywhere.

"In Ireland you can catch 20lbs pike just like that!" I remember saying once.

I failed to notice the effect all this was having on poor old Pud and his mother, Ma Pud. In retrospect, it is quite possible that I was an arrogant thoughtless little prig, serenely oblivious to the hurt I was causing to my dear friend Pud, who never went anywhere for his holidays, who had no uncle to take him to trout-infested stretches of the Nidd, who had no access to the fishing paradise that was Ireland.

School broke up for the holidays. As a parting gesture Pud received a beating from the thugs in his form, and our family prepared to go to Ireland. Pud was left to fish in the Brickworks pond on his own. He had no other friends and would be without my companionship for the next six weeks.

I visited him to say goodbye. I did feel a little bit guilty, I remember, and said something about bringing him back something from Ireland. It must have been incredibly patronising, because Ma Pud turned away.

As it transpired, that summer I caught no noteworthy pike in Ireland, only skinny little jacks of two or three pounds. The perch and the rudd were as plentiful as ever, but they were so easy to catch they became boring, and I scorned to fish for them. The truth was, that in Ireland in the 1960s there were almost too many fish. And anyway, I missed Pud's companionship.

My little brother Eck wasn't really interested in fishing that year and everyone else seemed to want to go car racing or horse racing. My fishing friend Noel had to help out in his dad's pub, and was rarely available. By the end of August I was glad when we returned to England.

As soon as we reached home, I got on my bike and raced round to Pud's house, eager to see him after all this time apart.

"Hey Pud!" I called, pushing open their back door.

His mother just stood and looked at me. She didn't smile or say hello, which was most unusual. The atmosphere was distinctly chilled.

I couldn't understand the cool reception I was receiving. For once, I felt like an intruder. I wasn't made to feel welcome.

Ma Pud, busy feeding the cat, glanced up and said something sharp I didn't quite catch, but along the lines of, "Come to tell us all about the big fish you've caught?" which wasn't like her at all.

Pud was upstairs, so I waited awkwardly in the kitchen with his Ma. As usual, the house was in a state of cheerful chaos – two dogs, three cats, a younger brother and a baby sister. Ma Pud was too busy to bother with me.

Pud came in and grinned ruefully. He, at least, seemed glad to see me.

"Hi," he said.

"Hi."

We didn't say much.

Ma Pud intervened. Putting down the dish of cat food, she stood and turned to me.

"Martin's been fishing while you've been away. Haven't you Martin?"

Pud shrugged uncomfortably, but said nothing.

His mother nudged him, but he merely looked embarrassed.

I spoke up, anxious to end the tense atmosphere. "Really Pud – did you catch anything?"

Pud glanced at his Ma. "Nothing much."

His mother pushed him forward. "Go on Martin, tell him."

Pud shied away.

Ma Pud stepped between us. "Well if you won't, I will." She pointed towards the back door, opening onto the porch. She seized my arm and led me to the door. "Go round the back and you'll find a bucket."

I didn't know what to say or do, she sounded so unusually irritated. I had never seen her like this before.

"Go on, look and see."

I led the way, mystified. Pud followed. I had no idea what to expect, but there, on the back step, was a bucket.

Ma Pud took my hand and directed me to the bucket. "Have a look at that."

I bent close. The bucket was full of water, and in the water was the head of a large pike. A very large pike.

"Martin caught it. In the Brickworks pond. Didn't you Martin?"

I looked at Pud.

He grinned shyly. "Yeah."

It was obvious from the hurt expression on his face that he was loathing every minute of this conversation.

Suddenly I guessed. The beginnings of adult understanding entered my mind.

I realised now the reason for his mother's sharpness with me. How I must have upset him and his mother with my endless tales of trout fishing on the Nidd, of the monsters I would catch in Ireland, and worst of all, my patronising comment that I might bring him something back. It made me squirm with embarrassment to hear myself saying those awful words, "I'll bring you something back from Ireland."

My only salvation is that at least I had the grace to understand how my thoughtlessness had hurt my best friend, so I clapped him proudly on the back. I wanted to share his success.

"How'd you catch it Pud?"

"On Grandad's giant spoon."

I laughed. "Really?"

"Yes." He grinned shyly. "It was a fluke really."

"No, no, it's a monster. Biggest pike I've ever seen! Well done!"

"Nearly pulled me in!"

Good old Pud. We were friends once again.

Even his mother relaxed. "Come on inside. I expect you're starving as usual. Fancy a cup of coffee and a biscuit?"

I nodded and we went back into the house together. I was forgiven. (Though I was careful never again to boast of my fishing ever again.)

One strange thing though, neither of us ever caught a pike in the Brickworks pond again. Weird that, wasn't it? Pud must have caught the one big fish it held and I must admit it served him proud. I always respected him for his reticence in not boasting about his catch – after all, if it had been me catching such a monster in such an unlikely place as the Brickworks pond we would never have heard the end of it, but not Pud. Typical of him, he just admitted it was a fluke.

Shortly afterwards, the town council realised belatedly that the pond was filling with water at an alarming rate and becoming a danger to the surrounding housing estate. The pond was drained and filled with rubble. Now it is the Municipal Amenity Tip and the haunt of hundreds of rats.

But to me it will always be where Pud caught his monster pike.

Supper is served

As a young boy, I had always been an avid reader of such interesting and inspirational books as *Coral Island*, *Robinson Crusoe* and *The Swiss Family Robinson* – all of which are probably banned nowadays as being too racist, bourgeois or literate for today's children.

Anyway, in those far-off innocent days, and as a result of reading the wonderful adventures of my castaway heroes, I always dreamed of living wild, fending for myself in some alien tropical environment, living off the fish I could catch and the fruit I could pick.

There being a distinct lack of such alien tropical environments in Yorkshire, I realised I would have to make my dreams a little more mundane and realistic. Back in Richmond I had once tried living wild, with only limited success, but it had taught me some valuable lessons. My choice of fellow savages had been unwise and had led to serious disagreements, amounting almost to murder and mutilation along the lines of the characters in '*Lord of the Flies*'. This time I would choose my companions more carefully and I would fend for myself in some alien environment closer at hand, like the Pinewoods, Hooky Wood or on the Island.

The Island was the best bet. The other two potential sites both had plentiful dog walkers and hordes of courting couples, which intrusions kind of ruled out the excitement of living wild.

The Island was isolated from both animal and human visitors. It was about five miles away on the Nidd between Goldsborough and Little Ribston. While lacking some of the necessities of a tropical jungle, such as sunshine, lianas, mangoes and of course coconut palms, it was nevertheless wild and overgrown.

It wasn't tropical and it wasn't jungle, but it was surrounded on all sides by water, was rarely visited by human beings, and was ideal for camping. Surely I could live off the land in such an idyllic place, with the river full of trout and hedges full of brambles, hazelnuts and countless other varieties of nature's goodies.

It wasn't an easy job persuading my friends that they should join me in the pleasures of being cast away on a desert island. At the age of thirteen most of them were weak, soft and suburban and I doubted whether they could survive life without regular infusions of pop music and television. Others were simply unimaginative and incapable of perceiving the delights which life as a savage might have for them. Eventually however, I succeeded in persuading my one close friend and two rather less close friends to join me.

First there was Pud, my short-sighted genuine friend, who was desperately keen to be a savage, but of doubtful competence. His life was one long Band Aid, as he was incapable of performing the simplest of tasks without injuring himself. Buttering toast usually involved bloodletting for Pud.

Next came Mad Willy – who was the most easily-persuaded boy at school. I had once suggested to Mad Willy that it might be fun to steal a flask of Hydrochloric Acid from the Chemistry Lab, and place it in one of the lockers next to the Master's desk in our form room.

My plan was that in a Geography lesson Willy was to sidle up to the Master, a kindly old gentleman known as Pop Weg, with some enquiry of a geographical nature. Pop Weg spent most lessons reading *The Times* or photography magazines, and he would hardly notice it when Willy opened the adjacent locker door and slipped his hand inside, a hand concealing a large lump of Iron Sulphide (also stolen by Willy from the Chemistry Lab.) Mad Willy would then drop into the acid the lump of Iron Sulphide, with the result that the very smelly Hydrogen Sulphide - known to us all as Fart Gas - would be produced in large quantities. I thought it was a hilarious plan, and one guaranteed to liven up the usually dull Pop Weg Geography lessons.

Mad Willy had obligingly done as I had suggested, causing an eruption and emission of toxic fumes beyond my wildest dreams. To my delight the cloud of poisonous gas had rapidly filled the classroom, had expanded into the corridor and along to other classrooms, and had caused an emergency evacuation of the entire teaching block. Mad Willy had willingly owned up as the perpetrator of the dastardly deed, and had smiled throughout the energetic beating he had received as punishment. He still remained eminently suggestible and wonderfully gullible. He went on to become a Brain Surgeon.

The last of the castaways was Babcock, a friend about whom I had always had doubts. At our very first meeting on the day I started school, he had announced that he was the most intelligent boy in the class and that as I was a New Bug, I was therefore vermin - after which we had fought a long and inconclusive fight.

We remained rivals in the following years. He was top of the class in some subjects, I was top in others. We were to retain this rivalry for years, fighting irregularly over trivial matters. Babcock was thoughtless, selfish, arrogant and unpopular. Nevertheless there was something vigorous and energetic about him I liked. Only when he went to university did our rivalry end. He discovered drugs in a big way and destroyed too many brain cells to ever recover.

Having formed my own gang of suitable castaways, I gathered them together one hot summer's day at my house. We were all excited at the thought of this adventure, which was to include an overnight stay in the wilds of deepest Yorkshire, the first time any of us had spent a night away from home without adults. At our house we packed together a large, but moth-eaten and much-patched tent provided by Dad Pud, a couple of pots to do the cooking in, and were all set for the off.

"What are you going to eat?" Dad asked.

"We'll be alright Dad," I scoffed. "We're going to live off the land."

How confidently did I ignore parental advice to take some food with us. Nevertheless, I pretended not to notice when my Dad slipped a can of beans into the saddlebag of my bike. With a cheery wave from my Dad, dire predictions of imminent death from my brother, and a tearful wave from my Ma, we set off on our bikes for a weekend on our very own Coral Island.

The river was low even for summer. The sun was hot and high in a cloudless sky. We stopped at Roger's Lido for our last contact with the luxuries of civilisation (a shared bottle of pop.) And after that it was open country all the way to Little Ribston.

We parked our bikes behind a hedge near Scalibar Farm and then set off down the fields to the river and our Island. We were in good spirits, Babcock slashing at passing vegetation with a large though mercifully-blunt sheath knife, Mad Willy singing inaccurate verses of '*I love to go a-wandering*' and Pud chewing thoughtfully on the remains of the meat paste sandwiches provided for him by Ma Pud.

I was already dreaming of grilling fat trout on the hot embers of a fire, the smoke lazily rising into the night sky, while midges danced above the water and the moon came up high over distant Birkham Wood.

Everything went smoothly, just as I had imagined. On the island we found an ideal campsite, well-protected from view. There was plenty of dry driftwood for our fire. The tent pegs stayed firm in the soft earth. It was perfect.

"Right then," said Babcock, when we'd pitched camp. "I'm off climbing trees. Anyone coming?"

Mad Willy leapt to his feet, keen for action.

"But what about catching our supper?" I asked.

"Ah, that's your department," beamed Babcock. "You're the expert fisherman."

I looked to Pud for support, but he only shrugged helplessly. Surviving off our own catches was my idea, after all. I could hardly blame Babcock for not joining in.

"Just get the one trout for me," Babcock suggested slyly. "I don't want to put on too much weight."

Mad Willy and he then smashed their way off through the undergrowth, to climb trees and play at being Tarzan. I could hear them whooping and hollering as they fought their way down the riverbank. Pud and I were left to tackle up and catch our tea.

Unfortunately, our tea that day was far from being co-operative. The combination of high bright sun and low clear water is usually fatal to good fishing, and so it proved. I tried, by God; I flogged that river up and down. I stalked fish, I crept on all fours, I sneaked up on dozing trout and dropped flies softly on their nose ends. Not a tickle did I get. The trout were all sunbathing, like everyone else around here. (There had been no Tarzan noises for a couple of hours, which I thought was very suspicious.)

Still, I fished on determinedly, conscious at every turn of the voice of Babcock demanding, "Where's my tea then?"

I abandoned the flies and resorted to upstream worming, and in this way did manage eventually to catch three fish. Unfortunately two of these were gudgeon and the other was a six inch dace – hardly a fitting banquet for four starving savages, but there you are. You couldn't have everything and we had had a wonderful day, temperatures in the 80s, never a cloud in sight, perfect peace and tranquility.

There was a crashing of bushes. "I'm starving! Where's my tea?"

It was Babcock, leading the other half-naked and equally sunburnt savage into our jungle clearing. I glanced at Pud and pointed to the two gudgeon and the six inch dace laid out at my feet.

Babcock took one look. "Yeah, that's okay for you. Where's mine?"

"That is yours. Or rather, one quarter of it is."

Babcock's dirty red face split into a sneer. "That's it? That's all you've caught for us!"

I could feel my temper rising.

"Two miserable minnows and a goldfish!"

"Dace," I corrected.

"Dace. Blimey, if I'd known this was all you were going to catch I'd have stayed at home. You said it'd be easy, you said..."

"Oh shut up Babcock. It's the sun you see."

"Bugger the sun, bugger the goldfish. I'm starving.

Aren't you Willy?"

Mad Willy bared his teeth and panted to show the depth of his hunger.

"If you've got five loaves…" I began.

"What?"

"Five loaves. I've got three fishes. I'll wave my hand over them."

"Don't be so stupid!"

"It was a joke dickhead."

He sat down grumpily on an old log, which promptly collapsed under him, spilling him onto the ground and destroying his credibility. Sullen silence descended on the campsite of the savages.

Pud was the first to break it. "Anyone got any ideas?"

No-one had.

Pud continued. "We'll have to think of something. We'll get malnutrition if we don't eat something."

Babcock pointed at me accusingly. "He said we were going to live off our catches."

"Never mind what he said. What have we got between us?"

A search revealed a packet of crisps and the small tin of beans my Dad had secreted in my bag in case of emergency.

"Ah!" said Babcock. "What is this? You said, 'Don't bring anything.' You said we were going to live off our catches…"

"Oh shut up Babcock."

"This is for emergencies," said Pud, holding up the can

of beans. "And this is a bleeding emergency."

"You said…"

The normally placid Pud retaliated. "Oh shut up Babcock!"

"Don't tell me to shut up you four-eyed git!"

"Shut it," I said. "Knob Rot."

That shut him up. The mention of his hated nickname (Babcock, Bad Cock, Knob Rot) was enough to send Babcock into paroxysms. A fight was only averted by the intervention of Mad Willy and Pud, who stepped between us.

"Look, this is getting us nowhere. Put the tin down Babcock, we'll share it," said Pud. He looked hopefully at the rest of us. "Now what else can we find to eat?"

"Tell you what…" I suggested, feeling I'd better try to restore goodwill with a show of initiative.

"I'll tell YOU what," muttered Babcock.

I ignored him. "Why don't you lot go and see what fruit you can find."

"Fruit? Yeah, like pineapples and oranges. There's gonna be truckloads of fruit, isn't there? Anyone want a banana? Coconuts?"

"Shut it Babcock. Berries, nuts, stuff like that. And while you're off doing that I'll get the fire going."

Even Babcock seemed appeased at this. Getting the fire going meant hard work, whereas going off finding berries was a certain winner – if they found none they could blame me. If they found some they would be hailed as successful foragers, and I'd be the mere drudge, reduced to doing the menial chores round camp. And we could eat.

The three of them set off, while I found the small dry

twigs needed to start the fire.

Half an hour later they were back. The fire had progressed to a pile of dead branches burning successfully.

"What've you got?" I asked brightly, keeping up the air of optimism for the sake of peace.

"Nothing." (Pud)

"Nothing." (Mad Willy)

"Malnutrition. You twat." (Babcock.)

I could feel resentment and rebellion stirring in the late afternoon heat. I'd read *Lord of the Flies.* I knew what happened to Ralph and Piggy when the spirit of barbarism took over from the spirit of logical reason.

"Right," I suggested. "How about a Hunt?"

"How about a Hanging?"

"I didn't know you could talk through your arse Babcock. You must tell us how you do it sometime."

Babcock contemplated taking a swing at me, but for some reason (cowardice??) refrained.

I continued. "There must be something we can eat. This place is full of birds… ducks… coots…"

"I'm not eating a coot!"

"You can bloody starve then. Like I said, there's ducks… pheasants…"

Pud spoke up. "Come on then. Let's give it a go!"

I stood up, aware that this was my last chance. Pud stood to join me. Mad Willy looked doubtful, but slowly joined us. Only Babcock was left. He had that look of sullen brooding resentment in his eyes, but he also had that sheath knife in his hand and the prospect of using it was too much for him.

"Alright. Lead on Big Chief Shitting Bull."

By this time in the evening, I reasoned, the ducks would be returning to their roosts in the bankside alders. If we crept up on them quietly enough, we might be able to catch one. (The catching part I left deliberately vague – I had no desire to trap, or worse still, to kill one of those lovely mallard drakes with the gleaming green necks.)

We split into two pairs – Pud and I to go down one side of the island and search there, while Mad Willy and Babcock did the same on the other side. Separating the two tribes like this was a good move of Pud's, as cannibalism seemed the most likely consequence otherwise. And Babcock had the knife.

Off we splashed through the shallows, happily barefoot through the warm water.

"Best bit of the day," I muttered to Pud, who grinned and bent to his task.

It was exciting searching sedges, never knowing when a duck might fly out at us in the dim light. Exciting, but unproductive. We worked our way round the island and joined up with the other two.

"Well Babcock?"

"Need you ask? We got bugger all."

Babcock slashed the air menacingly with his sheath knife. Who knows what might have happened next, had not Mad Willy intervened. He was just finishing off searching the last bit of his bank, when he suddenly leaped up and shouted, "Geddit!"

There was a loud whirring sound. Mad Willy yelled

again, and something flew flapping wildly out of a sunken tree, its wings beating the water. Willy, who was carrying a heavy stick, swished down instinctively with it. By some fluke the stick caught the bird precisely on the head and it fell, dead, into the water.

Babcock was ecstatic. "Got it! Bloody brilliant shot Mad!"

And we all ran splashing through the water, shouting, excited, shocked and slightly scared, to see what Mad Willy had killed.

It was a moorhen.

Whooping like savages, elated by the success of our hunt, we stormed back through the stream to our campsite, Mad Willy triumphantly carrying his trophy aloft (well, in his hands anyway.)

I was mightily relieved – we could live like Coral Island castaways after all. Even Babcock was joining in the spirit of things, talking cheerfully of gutting the bird, cutting its feet off and making them into lucky charms. He was that sort of boy.

"I never realised he was such a total prat until today," I whispered to Pud.

He nodded. Obviously you don't know what someone is really like underneath until you've seen him stripped of the veneer of civilisation. Now we all knew exactly what Babcock was like.

The last red flaring edges had gone from the sunset clouds, and it was now darkest night. The fire had died down to red hot embers and we sat close round it in the blackness, our dirty burnt faces aglow with happiness and sunburn.

I lay back and dreamed of building a tree house, while

the others discussed how we should cook our food.

Mad Willy was all for plucking it.

"Nah," scoffed Babcock. Having seen a creature killed seemed to have stimulated him into taking the lead of our band of savages. "Take too long. I'm starving now. If I don't eat soon I'll start hallucinating."

"Okay Smartarse," said Mad Willy tartly, for even he was beginning to tire of Babcock. "What do you suggest?"

"Roast it in mud."

"Bollocks!"

"It's what the gyppoes do with hedgehogs. Supposed to be delicious."

There was silent contemplation of what this might involve and what the results might taste like.

"We'll pluck it," the rest of us decided.

This however, proved impossible and eventually, reluctantly, we had to resort to Babcock's gypsy method. Babcock as the originator of the scheme was given the dead bird and sent off to make it into a mud pattie. Ten minutes later he was back.

"There," he said proudly, presenting us with two filthy mud-caked hands and a muddy lump the size of a rugby ball.

No-one spoke.

I put the beans on, just in case.

We ate it. We had no choice. After a long day in the hot sun and fresh air we were all ravenous. We shared out the beans – about six each – and passed round the grilled bird.

"Done to a T!" boasted Babcock, who seemed to have taken to savagery.

Done to a T it might have been. Cuttable it was not. I tried slicing it with my penknife in the manner of my dad and the Sunday chicken. The knife slid off the blackened mud and into my finger.

Instead we passed the food around by hand.

"You first," I suggested maliciously to Babcock. "You're the cook."

It was amazing how keen on life as a savage he'd suddenly become since the discovery that it might involve killing things.

"No problem!" said Babcock, sinking his teeth into the twigs and mud that encased the moorhen.

The rest of us followed suit. Gingerly, it must be stated.

Actually, it didn't taste too bad. When I did manage to find flesh that is. Hidden inside an inch of mud it was not an easy task. It tasted… well, it tasted muddy. It was also very chewy. In fact, no amount of chewing could reduce it to digestible matter, so each lump of flesh had to be swallowed whole. It was like eating a tennis shoe.

Mercifully, there wasn't too much of it. A moorhen isn't much bigger than a blackbird.

"Never tasted better!" announced Babcock, smacking his lips together enthusiastically. He finished off the last of the carcass, while we put out the fire and tidied up the site. Then he pissed on the embers and dragged Mad Willy to his feet.

"We're off to get another."

Pud licked the bean tin clean and I smiled to myself at the unexpected success of life as a savage.

It was a night never to be forgotten. Alone under the stars, miles from the nearest town, we lay surrounded by bubbling water. The only other sound was the lonely creak of a sleepy pheasant. There was nothing man-made for miles around, we were alone on Coral Island…

Then Pud was quietly sick.

Mad Willy started up from his bag and vomited spectacularly over his own feet.

Babcock leapt up, cursed, "You bastard Willy!" when he thought Willy had puked over his bag, then laughed like a maniac when he saw where it had actually gone. He'd have laughed all night long, had he not gone suddenly very quiet and very pale. Clutching his bottom with both hands, he staggered from the door of the tent.

"It's my guts!" he howled. "My arse is gonna explode!"

Oddly enough, I was the only one not to come down with the galloping trots. I felt no ill-effects from our meal at all. No-one could understand how I had escaped.

Perhaps it was something to do with the way I'd secretly spat out my bits of moorhen. I couldn't bear the thought of eating some creature we'd killed. Poor old Babcock though, he retched most horribly.

All things considered, I thought going native as savages on our very own Coral Island had turned out very well.

The Monster of the Beck

We padlocked our bikes together, out of sight behind the stone wall, my friend Pud and myself, and untied the rods from our crossbars. This was all the tackle we brought, so there were no bags to carry. We held everything else we would use packed into our jacket pockets, for we never knew when we might have to run for it.

We were fishing Crimple Beck, and Crimple Beck was a private trout stream.

Pud had a soft canvas bag full of tiger-striped worms from his dad's muckheap. I had a small jamjar to keep bullheads in. We hadn't bothered with fly rods today because it had been raining for the past three days and the beck would be high and brown.

We slid down the banks between overhanging trees, until we could see the water. Nervously we peered through, eager to begin, but savouring the anticipation, for better almost than catching a fish was looking forward to catching one.

Surprisingly, the beck was much lower than we had expected, though still coloured, presumably because the water ran off very rapidly on these gritstone uplands.

We didn't talk. We didn't need to. We knew what we were here for and we knew how to go about it. At fourteen years old we were good enough fishermen to catch real fish, but too poor to have the opportunity of joining a real angling club.

We were able to make our way stealthily upstream, wading carefully in the current. Wellies were enough on the beck, because there were only a couple of deep pools and we could always skirt the edges of these. Anyway, we needed wellies rather than waders, because we could run much more quickly in wellies, should the occasion arise.

Crimple Beck was very awkward to fish, and for a variety of reasons. It had a good head of trout for such a small stream, so it was a source of constant temptation to us. But it ran in open countryside down the Crimple valley, through very sweeping and exposed fields. This made it dangerous for us because we could so easily be seen.

The only safe fishable sites were further down the valley, where the beck reached civilisation, running past the bottom of several very large gardens, before entering the village of Burn Bridge. Here it passed a busy pub, the Black Swan, and then ran alongside a lane through the village. As the beck was only fishable in one or two secluded pools just above the village, we had to get to those pools undetected before we could begin fishing.

Without a splash we sneaked past the bottom of somebody's garden. We didn't know who lived in the large house there, but a man had once leaned over the wall, spotted us, said some very rude words and had then set his dog onto us. We were always careful not to be seen there after that experience.

Then there was the pub garden to negotiate – no problem there as it was too cold today for people to be sitting outside. Another twenty yards of wading shallow runs and small pools and we were there. The weir pool.

It wasn't much of a weir, but a quick-flowing tributary joined the main beck just upstream of the dam, and together they formed the biggest, deepest pool of the whole beck system. And naturally, only the biggest, deepest fish lived there.

Our hearts were thumping now. My legs felt shaky, because I was scared and because of what was ahead of us. For in the weir pool, a week earlier, on the hottest day of the year so far, we had seen the biggest, fattest trout either of us had ever dreamed of. Under the gnarled and bloated old willow tree, well hidden among twisted roots, old branches and river debris, lived the Monster of the Beck.

Pud and I had been exploring without our fishing tackle, when we'd found him. Then we'd sat enthralled in the branches, watching him cruise in and out of his fortified lair, a great shadow that sent our pulses thumping. Since then we'd raged and fumed at the bad weather that had kept us away, but now our chance had come at last.

We were there. The tree was exactly as it had been in so many of my dreams. The water was dark and bubbles of froth sailed down as creamy spots. Knowing he was under there now, under all that tangle, made him all the more fascinating. And now we were here to get him.

There was very little fishing space in the pool, so silently we scouted for positions from which to attack the Monster. It was soon obvious there were two sites – either you could stand on the rim of the weir in six inches of water and throw your worm upstream towards his lair, or you could risk life and limb by climbing into the old tree itself, and dangle yourself over the deep and swirling waters, somehow lowering your bait into the den of the Monster. Two positions only; two fishermen to choose.

"Toss you for it," said Pud, generously.

"Nah, you saw him first. You have first choice."

"Are you sure?"

"Yeah." I didn't really want to give him the weir, the prime spot, but I felt obliged.

"Right," he said. "I'll go on the weir."

I was disappointed, but it was only fair. It was much the better site, with an easy cast and room to play the Monster if he should hook it. Still, there was nothing to be gained by complaining, so I edged past Pud and headed for the ancient tree.

I had to fight my way through a bank of nettles taller

than I was. When I managed to get a hold on the tree to pull myself up, a chunk of the old bark came away in my hand, tipping me backwards into the nettles. I fell and sprawled about, nettling my face and my hands.

"Ssssh!" called Pud furiously.

Ssssh? It was alright for him, he hadn't been nettled half to death. And when I did manage to struggle back into the tree I had such difficulty that I could only get my rod near the water by poking it through a six inch gap in the branches. I found I was just about able to succeed in lowering my bait into the water, but God help me if I got the Monster on. I'd have no chance.

Bait. Now there was a problem. Dry flies, my current favourite deadly bait, were not possible as I hadn't got any. Today there was a straight choice of worm or bullhead. Worms were reliable and were usually successful here on Crimple Beck (where we'd often caught two or three trout each with them.) I watched Pud tackling up; he was way ahead of me and I could see he was using worms.

Well, okay, I thought. But I'm not sure our friend the Monster will go for a worm. A fish that big, he was bound to be a cannibal. I fancy he'll go for a bullhead.

I don't know if you've ever tried bullheading for trout. It works, but there's one big drawback to it, and that is simply catching a supply of the wretched bullheads. This often proves an extraordinarily difficult thing to do when you really need them.

Bullheads are ugly little fish which live under stones and they can only be caught by hand. You have to catch them in your fingers by lifting up stones and trapping the bullhead before it can squirm off elsewhere, as they are understandably reluctant to act as live bait for great big trout.

Normally, as we'd brought a supply of worms, I

wouldn't have bothered with all the trouble of going on a bullhead hunt before I even started fishing for the Monster, but today was different. Today I had a feeling, a lucky omen, that I should try bullheading in the weir pool.

I knew it was ridiculous, and merely making life difficult for myself when I already had enough problems – like the massive ancient willow with its great fat bole full of birds' nests. And the impossibility of landing a fighting fish while suspended precariously on a branch above an unknown depth of water, when you can't swim, while surrounded by twigs, leaves and hostile landowners.

Ach, I thought, stuff em all. I'll go and find some bullheads. It's a family trait.

I backed myself out of the tree and slid down to the shallows at the edge of the pool.

"You're wasting your time," scoffed Pud, as he saw me bending to search. "I'll have caught him by the time you get your tiddler."

"Just you watch your worm," I said.

Well if the Fishing God was watching over me as I searched, he certainly didn't make things easy. Could I find a bullhead? No. They seemed to have vanished from the beck entirely.

Normally I could get a couple of them in five minutes. Not today. Not just when I needed them. Someone might see us and chase us off at any moment. Worse still, Pud might land the Monster.

Where were the bloody bullheads?

It took me a quarter of an hour of lifting rocks and desperately scrabbling under them before I finally caught one. Even then the term 'bullhead' was probably flattering him. He was a miserable-looking specimen, the runt of the stream, a tiny pathetic half-starved little victim who had obviously been sacrificed by his larger relatives as a gesture of appeasement to get rid of me. I picked him up and raised him to my face.

"Well," I said, "You don't look much, but two-inch bullhead on my hook is better than no bullhead at all. So tough luck mate!"

Pud looked up from his worm-casting. "You doing any fishing at all today?"

I waved my bullhead at him.

"Huh! That's about all you'll catch. Do you want to borrow my landing net to land that beast you've got there?"

A reassuring thought was that as yet Pud had caught nothing himself.

I crossed back over the stream and climbed up into my eyrie. Doing this with my precious bullhead in one hand made it even more of an adventure. Over on the weir I could see Pud shaking his head and muttering to himself.

Right, I was nearly ready. I found myself the lowest thickest branch that would support my weight and tried to jam a foot into the fork of the trunk to steady myself. I wouldn't fancy my chances if I fell in here, I thought. There was no time for such trivial considerations however. The bullhead wouldn't live long, even though he was only lip-hooked. I doubted if I'd be able to catch another.

"Come on bullyhead," I exhorted. "Let's show that worm-trotter what you can do!"

And with that I lowered him gently through a gap in the branches.

When he was a few inches above the surface I stopped, checked my position and looked for the exact place I wanted. It was no use just chucking my bullhead in and hoping the Monster would find him. He had to go in the exact hole where the trout lived.

Below me there was a bay, formed by the circling roots of the tree I was wedged into. It formed a deep, dark, black hole, into which I carefully lowered my bullhead.

Small though he was, he wriggled enticingly enough, and sailed away down into those dark depths. He wouldn't have swum off so happily had he known what was living down there. The denizen of the deep. A cannibal trout.

There was a muffled shout from across the weir. Pud had a fish on!

I felt a wave of envy flutter through my stomach. He'd got him! The lucky so-and-so had got him, after all I'd been through and when I had felt such good omens too. Ah, what cruel luck.

I watched Pud, half-hoping his fish would escape. His rod curved. There was a splash. That was a lot of splash for a big old Monster, I thought. Maybe he hadn't caught him, maybe… yes, it was a nice fish, but not the Monster. I must admit it, I was relieved.

"Nice one," I called quietly.

He brought his fish in, landed it, looked up at me in my tree and waved.

You keep waving, I thought. I'm going to get the Monster and that's the only one that counts.

"Want to borrow a worm?" he called in a loud whisper.

"No thanks." I had my dignity.

I smiled knowingly, for I had faith in my miniature bullhead. Come to think of it, I wonder how he's getting on down there, hidden at the bottom of the pool. Not much sign of life, perhaps I'd better just bring him up and check everything's well.

No, I told myself. Don't. Wait and be patient. He might

be right in front of that big old trout now… think about something else… the Monster might be just sizing him up as a tasty snack.

Ah, the bullhead's probably gone and died on me. I'll have to bring him in and try to catch another.

No!

Wait!

I forced myself to look about me. From my precarious perch in the old tree I could see into the garden behind the stone wall. It was a very large garden with a summerhouse and a huge lawn. Even as I watched, a man came out from behind a distant hedge and started towards the house. My pulse started to race.

Stay calm, I told myself. He has no idea we're here. Just keep quiet and he'll never know.

No sign of movement down below… give the bullhead a minute or two more… you never know, he did wriggle invitingly. I'm glad I stuck to my omens… if I was a hungry Monster trout I'd eat him up without a thought.

I forced myself to count to fifty, then I started to wind in. There was no point in wasting time, especially not here, for we'd be in big trouble if we were caught. Anyway, the bullhead had been gone on a long and obviously fruitless visit. There was no point in wasting any more time.

There was nothing on, nothing other than the bullhead that is. I could feel his tiny weight as he fought on the hook. He didn't give up easily, I'd say that for him.

I wound up sadly, slowly.

I could see the little bullhead now as he rose out of the hole towards the surface. He was still wriggling, so I thought I'd give him another cast.

Then there was a great shadow, a split-second view of a bronzed flank, and a huge white mouth opened and swallowed my bullhead. He just vanished. One second he was there swimming, the next the rod was juddering heavily in my hand.

"He's taken it!" I shouted. I instantly wished I hadn't, but the damage was done.

My shouts must have alerted the man in the garden.

I clicked the reel bar over, dreading every sensation on the line, that lightweight wriggle which would mean the Monster had spat the bullhead out.

But he hadn't. The winding stiffened. I was onto something solid, heavy and powerful. I pulled gently. The rod jerked and twisted in my grip. The reel screamed as the huge trout pulled out line on his flight to his lair.

"I've got him!" I yelled. I tightened the strain on the reel and felt the Monster, a slumbering, immense and potent force.

"He's there! I've got him, I've got him!"

How was I to get him out? The hook was only a size twelve and might not have much of a hold. The line was only three or four pounds breaking strain, for neither of us had ever caught even a one pound trout here before today. Certainly I couldn't simply wind the Monster up and hope that the tackle would hold. It wouldn't.

"Hoy you!"

I nearly fell out of the tree in shock. The man from the garden was leaning over his wall, looking up at me in the tree.

"What the bloody hell do you think you're doing?"

I was so scared I nearly fell out of the tree, at the same time yanking on the rod in my desire to flee, jerking it upwards and into the branches above. I had the line taut to the fish, so this caused the Monster to rocket out of the water and into the air above me, where it caught in the branches. It must have got one hell of a surprise.

I could hear Pud shout, "Run!"

A big dog started barking. There was this fish, this Monster, this beast of my dreams, dangling about in the air in front of me, wriggling and twisting tantalisingly, dancing there about a foot out of my reach.

"I don't believe this! You cheeky young bugger!"

He grasped the top of the stone wall, and bellowed up at me. "Are you listening to me you little sod?"

I took one hasty and fearful look at the bloke, now clambering over the wall, one quick look at my old faithful rod, one fleeting glance at the water below, and jumped, arms outstretched, for the fish.

I got both scrabbling hands round his slippery body, stuck my panicking fingers inside his gills, and screamed, "Help!" as I hit the water.

I felt the rod snap between my legs, but I didn't care, I had him! So long as I had my finger ends in his gills I didn't care about a bloody thing. It would all be worth it, for I'd got him, I'd got the Monster of the Beck!

I don't know how I got out, or how I escaped, but swimmer or not, I managed it, managed also to run squelching back to the bikes without being captured - and then I was safe.

There was Pud ready for flight, holding my bike one-handed beside his, and we were away.

All the way home I sang and shouted exultantly, "I've got him, I've got the Monster of the Beck!" while Pud rode beside me muttering, "Jammy bugger. It must've committed suicide."

The Monster of the Beck. A day to remember.

The flood

By the time I was fifteen I was quite an accomplished poacher. I couldn't afford to join any of the local angling clubs, so I would fish wherever I could, just so long as it didn't cost anything. To this end my mate Pud and I constantly scoured the district looking for places to fish. Nearest of course there was the Brickworks Pond which had furnished Pud with his monster pike. Sadly though, that had now been filled in and was a rat-infested tip.

There was Birk Crag, where for a purely nominal charge (6d or a shilling) you could sit round a muddy pond and catch tiny roach. Not a very fulfilling experience.

There was Crimple Beck, where I caught the Monster of the Beck, but we had gone off fishing Crimple Beck after our narrow escape from the man with the bad temper and bad language to match.

A few miles away on the road to Wetherby there was Plompton Rocks, where an amazing geological formation had once lured the great painter JMW Turner. There was a big lake there and for a small fee we spent many happy afternoons fishing for roach, perch and the occasional pike. But we longed for more.

We began to roam further afield.

One day we were out on our bikes somewhere near Ripon, about ten miles from our homes. The river here is the Ure, and in these lower reaches it is flowing through fertile farmland and is slow-moving and very deep. Obviously it is a coarse fishery, with the occasional trout as a bonus, washed down from the upper trouty reaches.

We were using a map, one of those wonderful old linen Bartholomew Ordnance Survey maps, a work of art in itself. It had every detail and best of all, was coloured brown for high land shading down to green for low land, which was really helpful to us fishing prospectors, unlike modern maps, which have been simplified and have lost their colour.

I signalled to Pud and we pulled in to the side of the road for a break and to consult the map. It told us that the river hereabouts was in very low-lying land. This was obviously true, as the fields were very flat and level. The meadow we could see over the wall even had that spiky bog grass growing in patches.

I unfurled the map and traced out where we were. "According to this Pud, the river is somewhere just over there."

I pointed and we looked but we couldn't see it.

What we could see was that there were trees some distance from the road, a couple of fields away, and the river was probably lurking somewhere among these trees. On the map it showed that on the opposite bank was Newby Hall, which I knew was a magnificent stately home set in lush parkland, but we couldn't see that either. The woodland of mature beech and oak trees obscured the river.

"Looks promising," I said.

The same thought had occurred to Pud. This was a good place to fish without detection. We could hoick our bikes over the wall and hide them, make our way to the river bank without being seen and then fish without fear of being caught. There was no-one around; the road had very little traffic and there were no nearby farms or houses.

We lifted the bikes over the wall, made our way over the fields and reconnoitred the wood.

We were right. The river was here, among the trees. And boy was it impressive! Big, wide and slow-moving, and better still, totally unfished. There were no paths, no well-used fishing spots. We were totally surrounded by dense woodland, so we could fish in here and no-one would ever find us. On the opposite shore there were the woods of the Newby Hall estate, and no sign of either a path or of any fishing club notices.

"Perfect!" said Pud.

The following day we came with our fishing tackle, popped our bikes over the wall, quickly crossed the low fields and climbed up a little ridge into the woodland, anticipating an exciting afternoon and evening fishing in this newly-discovered spot.

One thing I did notice was that the ground underfoot was very marshy. Even among the trees there was a squelchy sound as we walked. The land was level all the way to the river, rising to a low ridge at the waterside. The river, slow and deep and quiet, slid silently by beneath this ridge of land.

We tackled up quickly, excited at the prospect of fishing in this new secret place.

I had my trusty 12 foot Accles and Pollock, a steel rod I was to use until 2019. (I left it in a bin near Lough Scurr in Co Leitrim, as even I had to admit that after fifty years of use the rust had corroded it beyond repair. Not bad for a rod I bought in 1963!)

At this time I was very keen on long-trotting, using a tiny quill float and the lightest possible tackle. I had even foregone my dislike of maggots to use single maggot as bait.

We were right about the fishing – for it was fabulous! I got a nice chub, then, and best of all, hit a shoal of roach.

Roach were becoming a rarity by then, and I liked to fish for them. Fine tackle, delicate bites, a good fight for the size of fish. I got one after another, it was just brilliant fishing! By evening I had landed over a dozen.

Then it started to rain. A gentle drizzle, a misty wetness that settled upon us, but which didn't bother Pud or me. We had our parkas, and just pulled them round us. We fished on. The fishing was exciting and we weren't going to be put off by a drop of rain.

It was some time later that I noticed the river was starting to rise. This was very gentle and not at all alarming, but it was definitely rising slowly. It was barely noticeable, but was edging up the bank towards where I was sitting. There was no doubt about it. Up in the hills above Hawes there must have been heavier rain than the drizzle we were getting here down the dale and the river was beginning to fill and to flood.

I was still catching fish, so I wasn't bothered about the rising water. I could see it wasn't getting coloured or anything, so I didn't for a moment consider there was any danger.

Some minutes later Pud called quietly. He pointed to the river. "River's rising fast!"

I nodded. He was right. The river was changing. Even though we were in a very secluded spot and no-one was around, I didn't want to make a noise. After all we were poaching. There was no need to be alarmed, as the water was still some way below the level of the bank where I was sitting.

By now it was getting quite dark. I could barely see Pud, who was ten yards down the bank from me. I was about to say something when I had a bite; I struck and was into a good heavy fish, a bigger roach this time. I landed the fish, unhooked it carefully and held it up so that Pud could see. He smiled and waved in acknowledgement. I bent down to place the lovely roach gently back into the water.

It was then I noticed that the river had suddenly and very quickly risen quite a long way. Wow. This was a bit alarming. Worse still, it was now swirling and powerful and brown, no longer the amiable and sluggish stream it had once been. Surging water was rising fast, already near the top of my banking - if it kept rising at this speed it would soon be over the top and into our gear.

I called to Pud, quickly gathered up my tackle and started to move back. I wasn't wearing waders or even wellies as we had come on our bikes, so it looked like I was going to get wet feet.

"Woops!" I stumbled. I had begun to hurry now as the water was lapping round my feet.

Suddenly I became really alarmed.

"Pud!" I shouted. "Come on! Let's go!"

Pud was already packing up; clearly he was more aware of the rising water than I had been. I stood tall, trying to remember our bearings. It wasn't easy in the dark and I couldn't really say which direction we should take.

We were on our ridge of land, a bank above the river. I turned back towards the way I thought we had come and to my horror saw that the field was now under water! The river had somehow crept round behind us and was flooding the low marshy fields we had crossed to get to the fishing. Our way out was under water.

Pud was splashing through the water towards me.

"Let's get out of here!" he shouted.

I didn't need telling. Between us and the road stretched the water, now a sizeable lake for as far as I could see. We would have to wade through it to get back to our bikes.

It was now quite dark. I stepped into the black water. To my horror it was at least a foot deep. Christ! I thought. This is dangerous!

I took another step and the water went up to my knee.

"Bloody hell!" I shouted to Pud, no longer caring if anyone heard us.

He was some yards away, level with me, and he was up to his waist! I could see that his rucksack was already in the water.

This was serious!

We had a long way to go, we were in water now up to our waists, no-one was about, we had no lights and worst of all no-one knew we were here. How the hell had we got ourselves into this mess? More importantly, how were we going to get out of it?

I pushed forward and forced my way through the lake, but this only created a wave. I decided I would have to make only slow and gentle movements, or I'd go under and drown.

The water was icy cold, but luckily it seemed to be almost still, there was no current, or we would surely have been swept off our feet to our deaths. The river had slowly, imperceptibly flooded over its banks and had just filled up the fields behind us. We were stuck in the middle of a lake of icy black water in the darkness of an empty countryside. We were in trouble.

Pud was alongside me now. "What should we do?"

"Not much choice. We keep going." I pointed my rod in the direction I thought we should take.

It was absolutely terrifying. Each tentative step we took we seemed to get deeper and deeper into the water, and of course we couldn't see what we were stepping into. It could have been a hole and we'd have been in over our heads and that would have been the end for us both.

Nor were we able to see where we'd left the bikes. There were no lights anywhere. It was completely dark now and the lake was just getting deeper and deeper. We seemed to be making no progress. I just had a general sense of which direction we should be moving in, and trusted to my instincts that this was correct.

Water was up to our armpits now.

Neither of us could swim.

We were fifteen-year-olds, both quite tall for our age, but if the water rose another few inches there was no way we were going to survive this.

The water kept getting deeper and deeper.

I was in it up to my shoulders now.

How much further? How much longer could we keep going? There was no-one to help us; we had picked this secluded spot for that very reason.

I took another step, and now the water was up to my neck. Any further and we would both drown.

Suddenly, at that absolutely critical moment, there was a light. Over there to our right a car swung round a bend. I could see both headlights. So that was where the road was! We had been heading in completely the wrong direction.

I turned towards the road and took another step, not knowing if I was going to go under water, not knowing if it was my last move. I glanced back at Pud, who was following me closely.

I raised my hand out of the water and pointed towards the car and the road. Pud too was up to his neck.

He nodded. I took another step. This was it. The water was up to my neck so I had to move slowly. One step at a time, never knowing if that step was going to be my last. I edged forward ever so carefully, pushing my feet along and feeling my way. All the time the water was rising, insidiously filling the fields around us. Another step, another few steps ……

And then without warning, I could feel the ground was firmer, the water was not as deep. I took another step. The ground under my feet was rising. Then another step. There was no doubt about it, the water was getting shallower. Thank God!

I had my shoulders out of the water now. I felt my confidence starting to return and I was able to move more quickly, so that soon I was only in water up to my waist. I breasted the water now, not afraid of making waves, a few more steps and the water was down to my knees.

Twenty yards away I could just make out the shape of the roadside wall. I splashed through the water, panting, excited to be free, knowing that after all we were going to survive.

I stormed ashore, and grabbed hold of the stone wall. I stood there gasping, leaning on the wonderful solidity of the stonework, getting my breath back, legs shaking, heart pounding, absolutely freezing.

I had never been so scared in my whole life.

Needless to say, we said nothing of our adventure to our parents, who were used to us getting back late. No-one commented that we were soaking wet or that we were unusually subdued. There wasn't much we could say.

This episode taught me one hell of a lesson though – and that was never to underestimate the tremendous power of water. The river had silently seeped up behind us without us noticing, then it had surged across the low-lying fields cutting us off from the road. In the dark, all alone, and without anyone knowing where we were we would not have stood a chance. Six inches more water and we'd both have drowned.

There was a postscript to our near-death experience. Many years later I was reading *The History of Knaresborough* by Arnold Kellett, a local historian, when I came across an interesting story. He told of the great disaster that in 1869 befell the Slingsby family, the local landowners. Sir Charles Slingsby had been leading a fox-hunting party across the river near Newby Hall, when a tragedy had occurred. Sir Charles and five of his companions, had been swept to their deaths while trying to cross the river. The startling thing was that this had occurred at the very same spot where we were so nearly drowned.

In 1865 my great grandfather Ben Clough had had a similar near-death by drowning experience to the one I had.

The Leeds Intelligencer of 14th January 1865:

A SAD FATALITY

More than once we have had to record the loss of life by persons trying to cross the river Wharfe with vehicles and horses. Another instance of the kind occurred on Tuesday morning last, to a man named Jesse Ratcliffe. Ratcliffe attempted to cross the Wharfe, then somewhat swollen, at Denton Ford, a little above Burley, with an empty wood wagon drawn by two horses. Ratcliffe, at the time of the accident, was riding on the first horse, and when nearly across the river, the wagon was upset by the current, which at this point was very strong, and the poor fellow was drowned, along with both the horses. A young man from Bradford, Benjamin Clough, was in the front part of the wagon at the time of the occurrence, and had a very narrow escape.

Since our near-death experience I have always had the greatest respect for the power of the river, and have always been extra-cautious when wading. Even so, a couple of years ago on a chilly March evening at Dacre Banks, I stumbled when wading, lost my footing, overbalanced and was swept downstream. It cost me my mobile phone and a wet wallet, but it very nearly cost me a hell of a lot more.

Rivers need to be respected.

The Leather Shop Man

May 1966 and the Half Term break was upon us. I was in the Lower Sixth at school and, mad keen on fishing as ever, I had arranged to go on a fishing holiday with three friends.

I had written to a farmer up at Hawes, who had a campsite, and had booked us in for two tents for the week. We were excited because Hawes, as all fishermen know, is on the River Ure, a wonderful fly-fishing river.

By now I was the proud possessor of a Hardy split cane fly rod, and how that came about was a story in itself.

I had always bought my fishing tackle from a little shop in Harrogate, called the Leather Shop. It was an odd shop, located in an alley next to the Cock and Castle pub. The Leather Shop did indeed sell leather goods, ranging from school satchels to dog leads, as well as fishing rods, tackle and bait. It was clear that fishing was the first love of the man who owned and ran the shop. I didn't know his name, but as I had been a regular customer for years, he always took time to have a chat with me. The truth was I didn't buy much there, as I didn't have much money, so it was usually only half a dozen flies, the odd cast or two, or rarely, some maggots.

He was an oldish man, I realised, with thinning black hair. Somehow I had a sense that he was not in the best of health. He was rather bent in the shoulder and probably not able to get out fishing as much as he would have liked, so when I came into his shop he always liked to ask me how I was getting on with my own fishing.

Whatever I'd been up to I would tell him, carefully editing out all references to my many poaching activities. He liked to hear that I was a fly fisherman and that by now I was actually catching trout and grayling on the fly, despite the fact that I only had the dreaded Japanese leger/float rod bought for me in Ireland all those years earlier by my parents. It was a terrible fly rod, far too soft and soggy in action, but it was all I had.

Somehow, I may have mentioned this to the man in the Leather Shop, but if I had spoken about the rod to him I had done it inadvertently. I certainly wasn't begging for assistance with my fly rod woes, so it was a great surprise to me when he raised the subject.

One Saturday afternoon, on my way from school to my Saturday job at the Grand Hotel, I dropped in to the Leather Shop, intending just to have a look at some of the proper fly rods he had on sale. I didn't have the money to buy any of them, but I just wanted to set myself a target, some figure I could aim to save for. It was nice to drool over the unattainable!

I explained this to the Leather Shop man. He went to the wall, where the fly rods were stacked ready-assembled and price-ticketed. There were all lengths, from seven foot six up to ten feet long, and by now in the mid 60s they were all fibreglass, then the newest material. (This was long before the invention of carbon fibre.)

"Try one," he said kindly.

I shook my head. If I did feel one in my hands I'd only want it all the more and I just didn't have the money.

"Go on," he insisted. "We're not busy. Take your time." There were no other customers, so we had the shop to ourselves.

He wouldn't take no for an answer, and unclipped one of the rods from its place on the wall, handing it to me.

"Try it for balance. It's got to feel right in the hand."

I took hold of the rod. I couldn't help but notice the

price handwritten on the little card attached to the first ring. It was way beyond my budget.

"Wait a minute," he said. "You can't tell the balance like that. Without the weight of the reel you won't know if it will suit you. You need the reel on the rod to get the proper balance."

He went to the glass display cupboard, bent down and took out a box. 'Hardy' it said. The best fishing tackle in the world.

He opened the box, took out the reel – a Hardy Marquis I think it was – and handed it to me.

I fitted it into the seating on the rod butt.

"Now try it."

I did as he instructed. I felt the grip on the cork, weighed the reel against the weight of the rod and grinned a great big grin. It was so much better than my own rod.

He was smiling too. "Well, how's that?"

"Miles better." I passed it back to him. "I'd love it, but I just can't afford it. Sorry."

He took the rod back from me and started to take the reel out of its fixings.

"Thanks for letting me have a go with it," I said, for he was a kind man to take so much trouble. He knew I didn't have the money, but letting me try one out was very generous of him, and the rod was something for me to aim for.

He fitted the rod back into the wall fittings, and turned to me. I was about to leave, when he stopped me.

"Tell you what," he said, "I've got something here."

I paused.

"It's not the latest rod," – he indicated the ones on the

wall - "but it's a nice little rod. Might just suit you."

I shook my head, regretting that I'd started this. "I'd better be going. Maybe one day…"

"No, wait a minute." He bent down behind the counter. "Have a look at this. See what you think."

He brought out a rod bag, a brown canvas one. It was obviously not brand new, because the bag had a small muddy stain, but it was very nearly new. More significantly, this bag had a black and green maker's tag. And the tag read HARDY.

Hardy

Alnwick

England

Only the Rolls Royce of fly rods.

He'd undone the string and opened the top now. Out came the butt, drawn out delicately and carefully by the Leather Shop man. The cork had a few tiny bites, where the hook had been sunk into the butt, but it was almost new.

Out came the rest… a beautiful split cane rod, a wonderful golden brown colour to the wood, varnished red silk, golden agate linings to the rings, a piece of pure fishing perfection.

He laid it on the counter.

While I marvelled at it, he drew out the second section. Equally beautiful, and such perfection. It was both stylish and fragile, tapering to an impossibly fine point and a jewelled top ring.

He lay it on the glass counter beside its fellow section.

"Hardy," he said. "Glen Beg. Eight foot of Palakona cane. What do you think of that?"

"It's beautiful, absolutely beautiful." I stroked it gently. "Just beautiful."

He smiled, seeing how entranced I was.

I came to my senses. "But not for me! No chance! I could never afford a rod like that."

"How do you know?"

I shook my head. "'Cos I earn five bob working Saturday afternoon at the Grand Hotel." (This was my Saturday job).

As I stood there, just dreaming of what it would be like to own this rod, he watched me closely.

"Go on," he said. "Put it together."

"No. I'd better not."

"Like this." He picked up the top section, indicating I should hold the butt section. "Careful. Don't force it. They fit just perfectly."

He put the two pieces together, slotting them softly one into the other. He held it out to me.

Oh my God. If there is perfection in the world it was that rod.

He handed me the Hardy reel. I fitted it into the butt. My hands were shaky and sweating.

"How's that feel?"

I weighed the rod in my hand, lifting it gently, imagining what it would be like to cast such perfection. It was so light and delicate, so sensitive to every touch. I turned to him and grinned. I hadn't words to express my feelings.

But it was no use. I couldn't possibly own a rod like this one. Reluctantly, I passed it back to him.

"Some day maybe, when I'm a rich man!"

He smiled and took the rod from me, hefted it in his own hand. He was looking into the distance, staring at the tip of the rod as if he had just cast out the line.

Immediately I sensed that he was no longer with me, but was once more a young man himself, out on the river, with this wonderful rod in his hand. He didn't say anything, he didn't need to. I could tell where he'd gone though, by the wistful smile on his face as he imagined he was once again back casting a fly. He didn't say anything, but the pleasure on his face said it all.

I coughed.

"I'd better be off," I said. "Got work at 2.00." I pointed to the rod. "Thanks for letting me try it out."

He didn't say anything, so I opened the door and left him, still staring at the Hardy in his hand.

It was two weeks before I came back to the Leather Shop. In the meantime I'd skived off all my rugby Games lessons and worked instead at the Grand, thereby earning an unexpected windfall. I was also unusually flush because my dad had given me a pound for helping him out by delivering election leaflets for him. He was a Liberal councillor by now.

For once I had funds and so was determined to spend it on something at the Leather Shop. Not the Hardy of course, as it would be years before I could afford such a rod; it was a rich man's rod.

"Hello son," said the Leather Shop man brightly.

I didn't know his name, nor did he know mine. He was

on his own, just pottering about.

"Just want a few flies please. Greenwell's and a few Tup's Indispensables if you've got them."

He lifted out the glass-topped display box of wet flies. It was divided into little compartments, each with its collection of a particular type of fly. I leaned over and began to point out the ones I wanted.

He surprised me by interrupting the process. "I've been thinking about you," he said quietly.

I glanced at the wall full of fly rods. Even the cheapest fibreglass rod was way out of my financial reach.

"Yes," he said, "I've been thinking."

He disappeared beneath the counter. Out came the fly rod. The Hardy fly rod.

"It's second hand," he said, opening up the rod bag.

I stared, mesmerized.

"So it's not as much as you might expect."

He undid the bag, took out both pieces and passed them to me. I took them reverentially. It was as perfect as I had remembered.

"Fit it together."

He watched as I did so with great care.

"It belonged to a gentleman," he explained. "A real gentleman. He'd just bought it, but then something happened and he could no longer use it, so he sold it back to me."

I wasn't really listening, just staring at the wonderful rod.

He handed me the reel.

Oh my God. I just drooled. It was even better than I

had remembered in so many dreams. Just perfection.

"It's hand-built. Up at Alnwick. Look." He showed me where the rod joined the butt. There was black writing and an AFTM number.

Neo Cane

Glen Beg

8'

6

"See that number." He pointed with his finger at the lower end of the rod.

There next to the butt was written…

N.E. 7231

"That shows it's a unique rod, numbered so it can be traced."

A unique rod. Hand-made. Individually numbered.

I prepared to pass it back to him.

"Nine quid," he said suddenly.

I must have misheard. Nine quid! What was he talking about? Nine pounds. A ridiculously low price. He couldn't possibly be asking only nine pounds for this Hardy split cane fly rod, this masterpiece of the fishing tackle world? No, it was a mistake. This rod was worth a great deal more, really, a great deal more. Nine pounds was a ludicrous price to ask.

I looked at his face for confirmation.

He nodded and smiled. "Nine pounds to you."

My mind was spinning. Nine pounds, only nine pounds! Why, that amount was nearly attainable! In a year maybe, I would have enough if I worked hard and saved it all.

I shook my head. "I'd love it," I said. "But I haven't got that much."

"Pay me what you can. Ten bob a week."

I was stunned, too shocked to reply. Ten bob a week. I could manage that - it was two afternoons working at the Grand. Ten bob a week!

I was absolutely staggered. This was just incredible generosity on the part of the Leather Shop man. It was madness. He couldn't be making any profit selling it at that price. He could surely sell it for so much more than nine pounds.

I had to make sure he wasn't just teasing me.

"Are you sure?"

He nodded. "Ten bob a week will do fine."

"Right!" I held out my hand. "I'll take it!" I shook his hand vigorously. He was grinning as much as I was.

"Will you take the reel too?"

"No, the reel will have to wait. I've got an old one and it'll have to do." I passed him back the rod. "Take this. I'll be back in five minutes."

By good fortune I had my Post Office book with me. I raced along Oxford Street to the Post Office, and took out almost my entire life savings. Three pounds seventeen shillings and sixpence. Two and six was left in the account.

Then I rushed back and gave it to the Leather Shop man, with the promise I would pay him the rest in ten shilling instalments.

And so I left the Leather Shop the proud owner of a Hardy fly rod. A split cane 8 foot Palakona, with its own identity number. Only the best fly rod in the world! Me, a scruffy penniless sixth former, I had got a Hardy! I squeezed it in my hand, I cradled it lovingly to my chest, unable to believe it was actually mine. I could hardly wait to show it to my parents, to my friends, above all, to use it.

To this day I don't know why the Leather Shop man did it. I've often thought about his reasons for making such a wonderful and generous gift. I can only think that perhaps he saw something of himself in me. I could see by the expression on his face when he was holding it that he was miles away, on a riverbank somewhere. He had just cast out and the flies were drifting downstream…

In his imagination he was holding the line tightly in his left hand, expecting any second that there could be the tug of a taking trout, hoping that he would be quick enough to strike and catch….

Or perhaps he was not thinking of himself, but of me and the use I would get out of it. He could tell how obsessed I was with fly fishing, maybe that was why he gave it away, who knows?

I still have the Hardy. It sits in my study beside me now as I write, fifty five years later. I use it every week of the fishing season and it's as good as the day I was given it, perfect, clean, undamaged.

Every time I go fishing and I unfurl the knot and open the bag I think of that kind old Leather Shop man, and when I take the two pieces out and slide them together I remember the day he demonstrated to me how carefully and precisely it should be done.

The rod always attracts attention from passers-by. No-one else in the club has a rod like it; they may have their expensive Orvises, their Greys and Wychwoods, their carbon fibres, but I have my Hardy. My split cane

Palakona. My Glen Beg.

When people see the glistening varnish, that superb golden brown wood, those lovely red silk ring bindings, they marvel.

'That's a lovely rod,' they say, even if they know nothing about fishing.

One day I was in the carpark of Dacre Banks cricket club by the Nidd at Summerbridge. The car boot was open and I was tackling up, when a fisherman went by. Seeing the rod propped against the car, he stopped.

"My goodness!" he exclaimed. "That's a beautiful rod!"

I agreed that it was. He then offered me a ridiculous amount of money for it. Not a chance. I would never part with my Hardy Glen Beg. Of all the possessions I have collected throughout my life it is, without any doubt whatsoever, my prized possession.

HARDY

Alnwick England

Neo Cane

Glen Beg

8'

6

N.E. 7231

No doubt the Leather Shop man is long dead and gone, but I can tell you my friend, your memory lives on, for to give me that rod you showed you had the spirit and generosity of a true fisherman. A gentleman. So here's to you! And to the coming season, when I will be out with my Hardy Glen Beg on the Nidd on the very first day.

N.E.7231
8 foot of split cane perfection.

Blades Purple Dun

Four of us fishing friends had decided to make the Half Term of our Lower Sixth year a real holiday. Not for us the delights of the seaside – we were going camping to Hawes in Wensleydale. We were all mad on fishing, three worm danglers and maggot trotters and me, a desperately keen fly fisherman of doubtful competence. Little did I suspect it at the time, but this was to be a major step forward in the development of my fishing skills.

Hawes is a stunningly-attractive little town at the very top of Wensleydale, built entirely of grey Yorkshire stone. There is a huge market place, with a chipshop and some other shops dear to our hearts – butcher, baker and fruit and veg shops. More importantly there were at least three pubs: The Crown, The White Hart and The Board Inn, all of which we intended to sample, for this was our first big holiday without parental supervision. We were only sixteen at the time, but the plan was for us to walk tall, talk in husky voices and ask confidently for pints of bitter.

There were two rivers to fish in the Hawes area. The main river running just at the edge of town was the River Ure, which ran down the dale clear and fast all the way to Askrigg, Bainbridge, Leyburn and Ripon, forty miles way. On either side of the river valley rose great Yorkshire hills like Great Shunner Fell.... It was a spectacular setting.

But there was another little river - Gayle Beck, which flowed right into the town from the nearby village of Gayle. This beck had trout you could see, trout you could lust after, trout within catching distance, and for this reason it lured us lads before we'd sampled the main river.

It was possible to stand at the bridge over the beck right in the middle of town and watch Gayle Beck as it poured over a steep waterfall into a deep pool beneath. Every passer-by stopped at the sight, for visible to all were the shoals of trout which swam so temptingly in and out of the waterfalls.

Everyone pointed excitedly.

"Look! Look at all the fish!"

The first night there we couldn't resist creeping up the beck until we were under the town bridge. From our secret hideaway we cast worms into the pools and watched as the trout darted out to investigate, took one look at our offerings, and darted back unscathed into their holes under the waterfalls. It was exciting but frustrating fishing and from then on we decided to stick to fishing the main river, the Ure.

There were four of us camping in two ancient tents, in a farmer's field just down the lane from the market square. There was Stanny, my old friend from Junior school; there was Pud, my mate from school and the fourth member was Keith, also from my secondary school, a newcomer to our fishing trips. All of us were sixteen years old except Keith who was only fifteen and even worse, looked to be only about twelve years old. I mention this only because his youthful good looks did not augur well for our chances of being served in any of the town's pubs, which after all was the secondary purpose of our fishing holiday.

We had pitched our tents right next to the river, where it swept around a wide bend. It was our intention to fish through the nights, so our close proximity to the water was vital.

It was May 1966 and the World Cup was coming to England, so not only had we got the freedom of a week camping without our parents, we had the football to look forward to, as well as hopefully sampling our first pints of beer. It was to be an exciting and memorable summer.

We were all keen fishermen, though as I said I was the only fly fisherman, the others being wormers and maggot trotters. I was desperate to try out my new Hardy fly rod. So keen were we to fish that we were all up at dawn the next day, fishing in the early grey mist long before anyone else was about.

It was an eerie scene, wandering through the fog, occasionally glimpsing each other through the silvery mist, a magical, unforgettable morning. This was long before the tourist coaches would arrive, disgorging their hordes onto the river banks and spoiling the fishing. This was idyllic.

After we had been there a couple of days, everything about the trip was going really well. We had managed to feed ourselves without getting food poisoning; we had only fallen out with each other a few times and we had even somehow survived the chilly nights.

In the daytime the weather was hot and sunny and we quickly warmed up. Soon we were all catching fish, small fierce upland trout. Well, to be accurate, the other three were catching fish, the local trout for some reason seeming to prefer plebeian worms rather than my exotic flies. So far I hadn't caught anything, despite my possession of the wonderful new Hardy rod. Still, the mood was good, our spirits high.

When the sun got too hot and bright in the afternoon, we abandoned the fishing and changed into swimming trunks, sailing down the rapids of the big pool on a couple of Lilos we'd brought with us. Great fun and very exciting and having an added element of danger as none of us could swim. We didn't mind, we were sixteen and nothing could harm us.

After supper it was time to try the pubs. Nervously,

chattering excitedly to cover our fears, we walked up into town, and stopped outside the first pub we came to. The Board Inn.

This was it. Our entry into adulthood. I went in first, as I was the tallest, then Pud, followed by Stanny, and last of all Keith, who we ushered into a corner so no-one could see that he was barely five feet tall and looked on this evening only about ten years old.

Like hardened drinkers, we sat and pooled our piles of coins on the table. I think we had about three and sixpence between the gang of us, hardly enough to get us legless.

I was sent to the bar to do the ordering. The barman, a stout gent in a white apron, was wiping the top of the bar with a cloth, but looked up when he saw me approaching. He didn't say anything. There was no cheery greeting, but this was Yorkshire, and I didn't expect anything so Southern as a welcoming smile.

"Erm," I began. I was nervous. This was only the second time I had ever been in a pub and it was definitely my first time ordering beer.

"Yes?" He paused in his wiping of the counter.

I cleared my throat, hoping my resonantly-deep bass voice would impress. "Could I have four half pints of beer please?"

The landlord, a middle-aged man of considerable experience, took one long look at me, then peered round the corner to have a look at Pud, at Stanny, and finally at Keith.

"Hop it," he said.

At the next pub, The Crown, we were equally unsuccessful. We didn't even get through the door this time, the landlady spotting us plotting at the doorway. She gestured to us with that by now familiar greeting.

"Hop it."

We hopped it.

Before we arrived at the third and final pub we had a conference.

"Look, it's cos we've got him, the midget," said Stanny, gesturing towards Keith, who looked only eight years old by now. I swear he was shrinking after each rejection.

"What do you suggest?"

"Leave him." He pointed at Keith.

"No." I was quite definite about this. Keith was a good friend and we weren't going to abandon him just because he was six years old. "It's all of us or none of us."

Dejectedly we turned our backs on the pub and headed back towards the tents, our dreams of alcoholic delirium dashed for the present.

It was then that Pud spotted the off-licence.

I nodded. "Give me all your money. I'll go in. You lot clear off so they can't see you."

I pushed open the door, a bell rang. A scrofulous youth no older than my good self appeared. He was chewing gum and had a copy of the *Beano* in one hand.

"Yeah?"

"Four pints of beer please."

"What sort?"

I scanned the brown bottles on display.

"Bass."

"Only got halves of Bass."

"OK, I'll have eight halves."

Reluctantly he put down the *Beano*, and started picking eight bottles from the shelf. I could hardly believe my luck at finding a moron in charge of all this booze.

"Yer gorra bag?"

"No." I hadn't gorra bag.

He pulled out a brown paper bag and slapped it onto the counter. Obviously he wasn't going to put the bottles in for me, as he was keen to get back to the doings of Dennis the Menace, so I did it myself.

Two minutes later I was outside. They gathered round expectantly.

"Well?"

I grinned and shook the bag of bottles.

So began a great night. After being out all day in the hot sun, living on a diet of bacon sandwiches and crisps, and being totally unused to alcohol, we were all pissed out of our minds on two halves of Bass. We sat late into the night around our campfire, talking utter nonsense and giggling frequently. Oh that such easy and cheap intoxication could have persisted through life, it would have saved me a fortune.

Then, the next afternoon, without any warning, came trouble. We were just tackling up ready for an evening's fishing, intending to fish well into the night, when a man came through the farm gate, walking towards us very purposefully.

Stanny nudged me. The visitor was a very businesslike figure, dressed in country clothes, and I guessed immediately that he meant trouble.

Now it so happened that by great good fortune I wasn't actually fishing at that moment. As I hadn't caught anything on my exotic collection of ephemeroptera, I had temporarily abandoned flyfishing in favour of worming. My beautiful Hardy rod was safely inside the tent and I had no rod near me, unlike the other three.

I was hungry and was squatting by our tent trying in vain to open a tin of Spam, the little lever of which had snapped off just when I was in desperate need of meat. When the figure of authority approached I did not therefore appear to be a fisherman. Maybe that was why he ignored me.

"River bailiff," he announced without ceremony. "Can I see your rod licences lads?"

I swallowed hard. Rod licences? Christ! I hadn't got one! I'd forgotten all about it. For the last three months I'd meant to get one, but somehow it had always slipped my mind. Now I sat there, heart racing, frantically chomping away on Spam, praying he wouldn't ask to see my licence, because I was well aware that the penalties for fishing without a licence were severe. Tackle was confiscated. My Hardy was at risk!

Luckily he hadn't noticed my guilt-ridden face, and busied himself examining the rod licences of the other three, who had all produced their licences and were therefore legitimate fishermen.

This evidence of corporate legality seemed to relax the bailiff, who didn't bother questioning me sitting gnawing at a huge chunk of Spam, which was just as well, because the fact I hadn't got a licence was written all over my face and if he'd asked me for one I would have been caught Spam-handed. I was a poacher. A poacher who would face a hefty fine and have his tackle confiscated. His beautiful Hardy rod! I was crapping myself and it was nothing to do with the Spam.

Having finished with the rod licence business, he looked around the three anglers. "Fishing permits?"

Luckily for us we all had permits for the week, having bought them in a shop in Hawes. They were produced for his inspection. His official business concluded satisfactorily, the bailiff at once became more relaxed.

"How's the fishing going?" he asked pleasantly.

"Just little trout," Stanny replied.

"On the fly?"

"No. Worms." Stanny nodded in my direction. "He's the only fly fisherman."

I was horrorstricken. 'Thanks Stan,' I thought. 'You've just dropped me right in it.'

The bailiff was bound to ask for my rod licence now. But amazingly he must have forgotten that he hadn't checked me to see if I was legitimate, because he just said, "Let's have a look at the flies you're using."

Clearly he was keen to help and give advice. I reached into the pocket of my parka and took out my fly box.

Now that I was no longer about to be arrested and lose my Hardy, I felt quite pleased to be able to demonstrate my skills. I was very proud of my fly-tying ability, all the flies in the box being ones I had tied myself. So far I hadn't used any of them successfully, and was having to worm fish with the others, but that wasn't the point. I was a fly-tyer, a disciple of Frank Sawyer, GEM Skues and all the other Gods of the fly-tying world.

I took the box over to the bailiff and handed it to him. He flipped it open. There were my rows of colourful flies, like rows of little feathery soldiers. I was so proud of them I couldn't resist a smile to myself.

In those early days of fly tying I had gone in for the

exotic – parachute-winged dry flies, big yellow mayflies, bushy palmer flies looking like test tube cleaners. I even had Daddy Long Legs imitations. Little did I know, but these were all flies you would never use in the stony-bottomed and fast-flowing Yorkshire rivers, where hatches of exotic flies were non-existent.

There was no doubting his surprise when he saw them.

"Well," he said with a smile. "You've got a right colourful selection there son."

I beamed proudly, mistakenly taking this as a compliment.

He brushed his finger over a large bright parachute fly, one more suited to a Southern Chalk stream than the stony River Ure.

"Did you tie them all yourself?"

"I did."

The bailiff looked at me. I felt now that he was a kindly man, not at all the stern figure we had first feared.

"How old are you son?"

"Sixteen."

He gave a big grin. "Well, for sixteen you're doing very well."

I felt ten feet tall at this compliment. And then came the unbelievable moment, a moment of pure good fortune.

"I'm off fishing tonight meself. Would you like to come with me?"

I was stunned. The others were too. Not Happy stunned. Jealous stunned. Disbelieving stunned. Stanny was making a face behind the bailiff's back. Pud was grimacing. Even Keith was making hand gestures. Of all the luck! And I didn't even have a rod licence.

The bailiff gave me directions. I was to meet him at him at five o' clock at his father's cottage in town.

"What's your name son?" he asked.

"David."

He held out his hand for me to shake. "Mine's Blades. James Blades."

I nearly collapsed at the name. Blades! James Blades! One of the most famous names in fly fishing. My heart leaped. I couldn't stop myself blurting out, "Mr Blades, are you the inventor of Blades Purple Dun?"

He smiled and shook his head. "Sadly not."

"Oh."

That was disappointing. I thought I'd met one of the leading lights of fly-tying in the whole country.

"That's my dad. You'll meet him tonight."

When he'd gone the others were quite rightly outraged. Not only had I managed to escape a thoroughly-deserved punishment as a poacher, I had also been invited fishing by a famous angler.

"You jammy bugger!"

"Typical Clough luck!"

"I'm gonna tell him you haven't got a licence!"

As I set off for my meeting with the Blades family, Stanny came up to me with something in his hand.

"Here," he said, handing me a piece of paper. "You'd better take mine."

Stanny's first names were David Paul.

He grinned. "Least I could do. If you get a biggun bring it back for supper."

I stuffed the rod licence into an inside pocket and went off for my meeting with the illustrious Blades family.

The Blades' cottage was in the centre of the town, in a stone terrace up a little courtyard. Some young lads were playing outside with an old tennis ball.

"Is this Mr Blades' house?" I asked.

One of the lads stopped and pointed at the nearest cottage. "That's me grandad's."

I knocked on the door, so nervous I rapped too hard and hurt my knuckles.

Someone called, "Come in!" so I ducked down and went inside the low doorway.

Inside was a tiny room with a coal fire blazing away, even though it was a warm May evening. James Blades himself was sitting in an armchair, having a cup of tea.

"Come in lad, sit yourself down."

I did so. I looked at him as he supped his tea. He was not a man to hurry things, a man in his sixties or seventies. A countryman, in old country clothes. I waited for him to finish.

Finally he drained his teacup. "By," he said with a sigh of satisfaction. "You can't beat a good cuppa tea."

He eased himself up out of the chair and came towards me.

"I hear you're a bit of a fly tyer."

I nodded, too overawed to speak.

"Let's have a look at what you've got."

I took out my fly box from my pocket and waited nervously as Mr Blades examined the contents. I felt foolish now, showing him these exotic flies of which I'd been so proud.

He didn't speak further, or give me any indication as to his feelings about my handiwork; he just looked at them thoughtfully. He was a real gentleman, I could tell immediately. The flies weren't right for Yorkshire, I guessed. They were ridiculous, gaudy, flashy, not Yorkshire at all.

He didn't say anything but went to a cupboard by the fireplace.

It was hot in this crowded little room. I was sweating.

"Round here you might want to try one of these." He opened an ancient and much-battered fly box. There were neat rows of flies, but all were very different from my exotic creations.

He pointed his finger to one row. "Snipe and Purple. Very skinny. Just a wisp of snipe hackle and one twist of purple silk on the shank."

I was astonished, they were nothing like my flies, nothing like the ones in the Hardy's catalogue. For a start they were flat, almost two dimensional, whereas mine were very bushy, great round hairy things like the brushes of a chimney sweep.

I noticed too that he didn't have many varieties. There were the Snipe and Purples, and rows of Partridge and Orange, which I recognised.

I pointed at a row I hadn't seen before.

"Half Stone," he said. "Just a bit o' tup's wool really."

My own box was full of twenty or thirty different types

of flies, but he just had the four types, the last of which was of course the famous Blades Purple Dun.

I pointed to the row of BPDs. "Is that the one you invented?"

"'Tis lad," he said.

I could tell he was very proud of his achievement. Blades Purple Dun. A famous fly, a fly used all over the country. A fly held in high esteem even by expert fishermen. I knew I was in the presence of a master, a man who had spent his life fishing the Ure, a man who had created a lethal trout fly and had it named after him. Some achievement.

"Of course," he said. "I'm not saying that yours won't catch fish, I don't know. These are just what we use round here. Try yours out, see what you get."

He had been careful not to put me down, such a gentleman. He could have taken the mick out of my gaudy monstrosities, but he didn't.

"One bit of advice though." He pointed out the rows of flies in his box. "I'd make 'em in a good range of sizes."

I looked carefully. In his box there were 12s, 14s, 16s, even 18s.

"Tek two of each size in case you loss one. Best to be prepared. You never know what they fancy. Bigguns, small uns. Best to be prepared."

I thanked him, and to my surprise he held out his hand and handed me an old crumpled envelope. I peeked inside. There were half a dozen flies. James Blades was giving me a selection of his own personal flies!

"Tek 'em," he said, "And good luck."

I nodded, conscious that I was in the presence of a famous fisherman and that this was advice I would never forget.

Generosity, the spirit of a real fisherman.

His son had arrived by now and we set off in his van, out of Hawes, down the main road towards Bainbridge. A few miles out of town we turned down a bouncy little farm track, which led us right to the river's edge.

We clambered out and looked at the water. The first thing I noticed was that it was a much bigger river here than in Hawes itself; other becks must have joined it and swelled its volume. Here it was three or four feet deep, running fast and wide between completely open banks. There were no trees at all, for we were in wild, bare countryside. All we could see around us were the fells, the stone walls and sheep.

We tackled up together, Mr Blades finishing first. He watched me get ready, but made no comment about my equipment.

"Right lad, let's see if we can catch some fish."

We separated, him going upstream and me heading downstream. I didn't take any notice of this, being so desperately keen to get fishing with my new rod and to impress my illustrious companion.

I was fishing my usual method: three wet flies, fished down and across. I had waders by now so I could stand in the water and cover most of the river. The Hardy rod was just perfection. With the gentlest of flicks it would cast beautifully. With this rod it was easy to send the flies to the far bank.

I enjoyed casting a long line in those days, thinking that was the best way to catch fish. How wrong I was.

I caught two fish, but both were grayling, easier to catch than trout and not as wily or cautious.

After an hour Mr Blades came and sat down on the bank nearby. I could tell he was watching me, but he made no comment as I fished, always down and across, down and across. I took pride in casting a long line, secure in the knowledge that by now I was a half-decent caster of a fly line.

"Come ashore lad," he said after some time. "We'll have a cuppa."

He waited as I waded back across the river and scrambled up the bank. He had poured two cupfuls out of a thermos flask and passed one over to me as I sat down beside him.

"Have you caught owt lad?"

"Two grayling."

"Okay, that's a start. But we're really after trout aren't we?"

"Yep."

"Right then, let's have a look at your tackle."

I pulled in the cast and showed it to him. Black Spider as top dropper, Greenwell's Glory on the middle dropper and Gold-Ribbed Hare's Ear at the point. I waited for the verdict.

"Nowt wrong with your flies."

He pulled my rod over to him and examined it closely. "Lovely rod."

I puffed with pride.

He pulled the cast close and ran his finger along it up to the fly line.

"Line's fine. Kingfisher, same as mine. Mebbe your cast's a bit heavy, try a lighter one next time."

He put down my rod and pulled his own rod close.

"Have a good look at mine."

It was fibreglass and a bit longer than mine, but there was nothing outstandingly different about it.

He took hold of the cast and held it out for me to inspect. "This is what we do round here. Not saying there's owt wrong with your method, but this is what we use."

His cast was very different from the one I was using. I noticed first that it was very short, only six foot at a guess, rather than the nine-foot-long casts I used. The droppers were both very short too, only two or three inches long, not the nine inch ones on the casts that I bought from the Leather Shop. His had been cut short deliberately. This made the flies very close together, on very short droppers.

The flies themselves were the very sparse ones his dad had showed me. There was barely anything to them and a far cry from my colourful and fantastic creations.

"We fish two wet flies like you've been doing." He pulled the top fly up close. "But the top dropper we fish dry."

He held it up. It was a tiny Ginger Palmer. This was a surprise.

"Palmer for top dropper, and fish it dry. And," he took out a tiny pair of scissors, "We clip the hackle."

I could see now that the hackle had been trimmed, so that the ends of the feather weren't the natural sharp points of a cock feather, but blunt stumps.

"Sits better," he explained. "Floats nice and you can see it. It'll act like a float indicator."

This was a complete revelation to me. I had never

heard of fishing like this. It wasn't in any of the trout fishing books I had ever read.

"Cast upstream. Right and Left. Nice short line. You don't need to do long casts. If you wade quietly you'll creep up on 'em and you won't need to cast a long line."

It was a lot to take in, a complete revision of everything I'd learned so far about fly fishing.

"And one last bit of advice. Fish 'em upstream. Keep the line short and keep in touch with your flies. Upstream. They'll come back to you quickly in fast water like this. That's why the cast's so short and the droppers are short too. Stops 'em tangling."

He patted me on the shoulder. "Give it a go lad, you're halfway there already!"

I didn't know what to say. I had been doing everything wrong – from the ridiculous flies I was using, to the over-long droppers, to the lengthy casts and worst of all, to my method of fishing Down and Across. I was a complete disaster.

I was embarrassed, but after a few moments I realised he was a kind man and hadn't pointed out my faults, instead he had just gently shown me his methods and left me to draw my own conclusions.

Fortified with his encouragement I was ready to try his suggestions for myself.

We sat for the next ten minutes while I changed my tackle. I cut off the long nine-footer, trimmed the droppers and changed the top fly for a Ginger Palmer.

He lent me his scissors and watched as I snipped the edges off. Then he lent me his dry fly lotion, and we waited until it dried. Some Mucilin to grease the end of the leader and I was ready.

"Good lad. Shows you listen. Always a good thing."

I stood and the pair of us walked back to the river. Before we got close, he held me back and crouched low, indicating I should copy his method. Instead of launching myself into the water like the battleship Bismarck, I edged my way in slowly and quietly, remembering what he had said about wading carefully so that the fish weren't scared off.

"Right lad, away you go!"

I let out line carefully and quietly, and started to false cast. I did as I had been told, fishing upstream, right and left on a short line and keeping in touch with the flies.

In half an hour I caught two fat trout, using the methods he'd taught me! I couldn't stop smiling, so pleased was I.

In one evening with an expert fisherman I'd learned more about fly-fishing than I'd learned in all my years of trying. I was so grateful to him that next day I went into the grocers and I bought him a box of chocolates, a tennis ball for his lad and a packet of tea for his dad.

And I've been using his methods ever since.

Thanks Mr Blades.

Both of them.

Sex and fishing

Sex and fishing don't mix. Don't even try to combine the two. I know now, as a mature adult, that they don't mix and never will mix, but I had to learn the hard way, through many bitter experiences.

Of course, I only learned this important axiom as I got older. As a teenager I was as full of lust and idiocy as all teenagers are, and I often tried to combine two of my favourite interests, fishing and sex – though without any conspicuous success in either. Occasionally I was lucky with my fishing; sometimes I was lucky with my girlfriend, but never was I lucky with both at the same time. That is, until I met Arcadia…

Arcadia Hebblethwaite was her name. I met her in a bus queue, so it was obviously ordained in Heaven. I was sixteen and at an all boys' school. She was sixteen and at the mixed Grammar school in nearby Knaresborough. We had a lot in common. Lust. And it was my earnest intention to have a lot more in common.

Her main attributes were two immense breasts and a lion's mane of blonde hair. So far I had only touched the latter as there wasn't much opportunity in the bus queue for the former. This failure was, I was certain, more owing to lack of a suitable opportunity than to lack of enthusiasm on her part. She seemed willing enough. I could tell by the subtle way she rubbed herself up against me before getting on the number 16.

I realized that matters were coming to an exciting head when one day she slipped something into my hand as we queued together. It was a pop record. At first I was baffled, but she smiled knowingly and squeezed my hand with hot-blooded enthusiasm.

When I reached home I raced up to my bedroom and took out the record. It was '*Making Love*', by 'Floyd Robinson'.

Still baffled, I put the 45 on our little player. The lyrics had a surprise for me:

What would people say?

What would people do?

What would people think

If they knew I was with you

Instead of being off to school

I was with you, Making Love,

Making love, Making love…

Hmm, I thought, I wonder what she's trying to tell me. (I told you sixteen-year-old boys can be remarkably stupid.) But even I, gauche and gormless as I undoubtedly was, finally understood that this song might be a subtle hint that she was keen for our relationship to make some physical progress.

What we needed now was some privacy, somewhere secluded where we could be alone. Her own house was out of the question. Her mother had a droopy-eyed Basset hound, which always molested my ankles until it got an erection. It would never leave me alone long enough for Arcadia and I to get to grips with each other and its red-eyed horniness always put me right off. My own house was out of the running too, as it was never empty and my brother Eck would want to spy on us anyway.

Time was also a problem. I had very little free time in the Sixth Form at school. We had lessons five days a week and on Saturday mornings. On Saturday afternoons and evenings I worked at the Grand Hotel and on Sundays and weekday evenings I was supposed to be studying for my A levels for university entry, though I usually went fishing instead. The only free time I had therefore was during my school hours.

Luckily, we had an easy time in the Lower Sixth. The official powers-that-be had largely left us to our own devices in a wooden shack on the edge of the school property. This was known as the PS Hut – PS standing for Private Study – a cheerful if naïve piece of optimism on the part of authority if ever there was one. For Private Study was unsupervised.

After lunch, instead of doing Private Study, several of us would abscond through the windows of the PS Hut, nipping over the hedge and heading for the bright lights of town. Indeed, a whole gang of us, me included, had part-time jobs in the local hotels on our Games afternoons. The school staff didn't seem to notice our absence; in fact I managed to get through my entire Sixth Form sporting career without ever once playing rugby, even though it was compulsory and held on three afternoons a week.

If we weren't working as waiters in the hotels, it was our habit to go fishing. What better opportunity could there be for me to further my relationship with Arcadia Hebblethwaite than down at the riverbank? The combination there of sun, fresh air and total privacy would surely free her of the restraints which had so far cursed our courtship (her bloody Basset hound, her mother, the other people in the bus queue.)

Eventually, after several lengthy and expensive phone calls and after a lot of difficult negotiation, I succeeded in persuading Arcadia that she should accompany me on a fishing trip down to the river.

"But what for?" she asked.

"So I can show you my tackle!"

She giggled. "Oooh, you are a one!"

"Yes, I am aren't I?"

She wasn't too bright. But she was a lot of fun.

I knew a place, a sandy beach on a hidden bend in the River Nidd near Little Ribston, where we could hopefully further our relationship. So far all the information I'd had on sex was a Biology Practical where we got to dissect some dead rats. The moment of high drama in the lesson was being able to identify and measure a rat's testicles. Not a high point in my sex life, it has to be said.

Naturally I hadn't apprised Arcadia of these reasons for our visit to the river – instead I extolled the virtues of nature, thrilled to the call of wild birds, enchanted her with tales of fresh air and privacy, and to use a particularly noxious phrase current at the time, assured her it was 'somewhere we can get our heads together.'

"Okay," she said. "But bring some rubbers."

Ho ho, I chuckled gleefully as I packed my bags for school next morning. With a bit of luck we'd be getting more than our heads together.

I sometimes cycled to school, so it would be simplicity itself to duck out of the PS Hut window after lunch, make my way to the bike-sheds and cycle home. Both my parents would be out at work, so all I would have to do was collect my fishing tackle, a very necessary groundsheet and blanket, douse myself with Brut aftershave and I was away.

The plan was that I would meet up with Arcadia in Knaresborough bus station (I knew all the most romantic places.) I would leave my fishing tackle at my mate Pud's house, and saunter home afterwards as if knackered out from a hard day's grind at my A level texts. Crafty eh?

Cycling in a heightened state is both difficult and painful, but apart from that, everything worked out as planned. I escaped out of the PS Hut window, helped on my way by an anxious group of friends, with such generous gestures as…

"Take my camera with you in case she gets 'em out!"

"Marks out of two? I'd give her one!"

And from the Boarders, "Tell us how you get on. We want details."

This last pathetic plea was from the Boarders, a pitiful collection of sex-starved youths wracked by years of self-abuse. They were only allowed out of school once a term, for two hours on a Saturday afternoon, so their knowledge of girls was entirely photographic. Most of them didn't talk to a female of their own age until they left school and went to university. I am convinced that their entire lives were warped by being incarcerated in this cruel fashion.

Back now to Knaresborough bus station, where at two o' clock I was standing waiting for Arcadia. No sign of her. Half two. No sign of her. Three o' clock came and went in a cloud of red buses and diesel fumes, but with no sign of the maroon and green blazer of Arcadia Hebblethwaite. She would be instantly recognisable, I consoled myself, as there was no chance of her ever being able to draw her blazer buttons tight across that chest.

I passed the time by savouring the fantasy which had been haunting me for weeks (and the minds of a significant number of Boarders too, I suspect.) For a small fee I had been entertaining them during Private Study lessons with wholly fictitious accounts of my sexual adventures with Arcadia.

In this fantasy, the scene is hot and sunny. We are on the beach by the river. We are surrounded by dense foliage.

The beach is soft and sandy. Strains of *Desert Island Discs* waft through the undergrowth.

Arcadia is sunbathing. Then the heat becomes too much for her.

"Fancy a dip?" she says.

"I haven't brought a costume," says I.

"Nor have I," she replies, lifting her blouse over her head.

Details after that always become somewhat hazy. The Boarders yell for more. I extract more money from them.

She never turned up, did she, the silly cow.

"I thought you were joking," was her pathetic excuse.

"Of course I wasn't bloody joking!"

"Oh. Sorry."

Did she have any idea of the damage she had done to my image at school? Christ, I had to take some stick the next day when the drooling Boarders came up to me for details, tongues lolling.

"Well, how did you get on then?"

"Left leg first? Arf arf."

I tried spinning some yarn about ours being a relationship forged on a higher plane.

"Bollocks to that!" they howled. "Did you get your end away or not?"

When I finally had to admit that she had stood me up, then the cries of the bitterly-disappointed and sexually-frustrated were loud and sorrowful.

"I bet he made it all up."

"She probably found out that he's homosexual."

"What a tosser!"

And cruellest of all…

"Who ever heard of a woman called Arcadia Hebblethwaite anyway? That just had to be an invention!"

She wasn't an invention. She was flesh and blood. A lot of flesh and blood. The only way to recover my self-esteem was to try again, so, nothing daunted, I did just that. Same girl, same place, same intentions – but this time, two weeks later, she showed up.

"I hope you haven't got any of those filthy maggots," were her first words on seeing my fishing tackle.

See what I mean about sex and fishing not mixing? Here was I, breaking dozens of school rules, damaging my prospects of educational advancement, risking terminal ridicule at the hands of the Boarders, and all set to sweep her off her feet to some romantic hideaway by the river and what do I get from her?

"I had to miss my dinner for you. Can we get a bag of chips before we go?"

But I am made of sterner stuff than many a man. I'm not to be put off by a couple of minor setbacks, nor by the Ribston bus being late, nor by the fact as I sat there outside the chippy watching her guzzle chips, my uncle drove by, gawped in amazement at seeing me five miles away from my own school during school time, before speeding off in a cloud of blue smoke, no doubt to inform my father what sex-crimes I was contemplating.

I even had to put up with her munching her way through the bag of stinking fish and chips all the way to Little Ribston. Boy, she could eat.

I even ignored the snide wisecracks made by the bus driver as he dropped us off by a dense hedgerow, out in the fields miles from anywhere.

"Nature Study is it then?" he asked, with an ostentatious wink and a leer in Arcadia's direction.

I affected deafness as he said to Arcadia, "Be careful when he asks you to hold his rod for him!"

"What a coarse plebeian chap," I said fondly to her to cover his ribald remarks.

"I thought he was okay. Quite fanciable in fact," said Arcadia. She had by now finished her fish and chips and was licking her lips.

The bus drove off, leaving us standing among bushes at the roadside. All around us were fields and hedges. In the distance was the river.

"Where're you taking me?" She looked at the verdant undergrowth and curled her luscious lips in disgust. "Not down there I hope!"

"It's not far."

She pointed at the thicket of spiky brambles. "I'll ladder me tights."

I groaned. Was there no end to her prosaic mind?

I groaned again.

She heard me. "You should have had some of them fish and chips with me if you were hungry."

I led her off down the side of a field.

Things went from bad to worse. There were now two weeks' more summer vegetation than when I'd first planned to bring her here. We had to struggle through waist-high corn and shoulder-high weeds. I had to thrash my way through a Malaysian jungle of giant rhubarbs and Old Mans' Beard, all of which really excited Arcadia, I could tell.

By the time we'd reached our secret secluded romantic spot she had been stung by nettles, prickled by thistles, shat on by pigeons and torn by corn. She was clearly not in the mood for love. I'm perceptive like that, I could tell by the way she stood there with her hands on her hips, looking down at her legs, legs which were all wet and slimy with cuckoo spit.

Somehow I sensed that her next move was not going to be ripping open her blouse. Even a born optimist like me realised it was time to concentrate on my fishing.

As it turned out, I had quite a good afternoon's fly fishing. Arcadia sat in the undergrowth hugging her knees, with a fixed, glassy stare. Occasionally she would break off to swat pointlessly at flies, or to cry, or to shout abuse at me. But I took no notice. By then I'd given up trying to mix fishing and sex and had returned to my first choice.

I managed to get a nice trout of well over a pound on an experimental fly I'd just invented. I christened it '*Arcadia*' after my erstwhile girlfriend, though later I changed its name to '*The Grizzler*'. As grizzling was what she had done all day I thought I might as well commemorate the occasion.

So it wasn't such a bad day after all. I caught a nice trout, invented a successful new fly, failed with a woman and got myself sunburned. All part of life's rich tapestry my boy, all part of life's rich tapestry.

There was a postscript to this story. When the inevitable retribution descended upon me (my uncle having ratted on me to my father, as I'd known he would) and I was called before him to explain exactly what I was doing in a bus station during school hours watching a Grammar school girl with immense breasts eat chips, when I should have been locked away at school with my A level texts, my Dad just laughed and said…

"Funnily enough, I used to take girls down there myself when I was your age."

"Really Dad?" I said with a grin, (sensing an escape from punishment if I could only get him to continue.)

"Yes… she was a vicar's daughter if my memory holds true. Just before the war…." He smiled at the memory. "Lovely weather it was."

"Never mind the weather report. What happened?"

"It was all very embarrassing… yes, very embarrassing."

"Get on with it."

"Well, as you know, the road runs right by the wood, and that's where we were, just under the hedge at the side of the Ribston road. I was just enjoying the first moments of sexual congress under the hedge in that meadow…"

"I know it well."

"…when I was suddenly conscious of being watched. Imagine my surprise therefore when I looked up and saw above the hedge the entire top deck of a double decker bus, all of the passengers peering down at my bare bum."

"Why had the bus stopped?"

"I have no idea. I don't know who was the more surprised, me or the passengers."

"What did you do?"

"Continued with the heavenly delights of course. She

had her eyes shut so she hadn't seen the bus and I thought it rude to upset her unnecessarily. Very sensitive girl. Vicar's daughter you know…"

"So you said."

"…which brings me back nicely to the subject of retribution. I think we'd better call a halt to the educational fishing trips, don't you? Just until the A levels are out of the way."

"Fine by me Dad."

"Good lad. Did you er…"

"No. I got a good trout though. And I invented a fly."

"I should stick to the fishing then if I were you. In my experience fishing and sex don't mix."

How true Dad, how true.

Hartley

Hartley was a nice lad. That's all you could say about him. He wasn't offensive, no-one disliked him, he was a nice lad. He wasn't particularly bright, but he was in the sixth form with me so he wasn't stupid. He was just a nice lad.

He was quite good at rugby, not very good at cricket. He was never in any trouble. He never did anything to break the rigid school rules. Never challenged authority. Never questioned anything he was told. In short, he was a conformist.

At the time I was about to become a student rebel. I was currently debating whether to be a Bakuninite or a Kropotkinite or just a plain old Anarcho-Syndicalist, so a conformist like Hartley wasn't likely to be a close companion to an urban revolutionary like my good self.

I didn't particularly like or dislike him, he was just there on the edges of school society, never a leader, never one to initiate anything, never doing anything adventurous or exciting. He was just Hartley.

I was surprised therefore when one day he said to me, "You're keen on fishing, aren't you?"

I said I was.

"My grandad's died."

I gave the conventional response, wondering where this was leading.

"He was a keen fisherman too."

"Right."

Was he going to pour out his heart to me, to share his grief? What was all this about? I was baffled.

"We're clearing his house. My mum's just going to throw his stuff out, I wondered if you'd like any of it."

Wow. This was a bombshell. I felt guilty now for not being nicer to Hartley.

We arranged that I should call for him on Sunday afternoon and we would go round to his Grandad's house, where his parents were busy clearing his possessions prior to selling the place.

I hadn't met his parents before. The father was polite and said 'hello.' He was very busy, carrying cardboard boxes out to the car. He was a civil servant, Hartley had said. A grey-haired man, quiet and unprepossessing. A grey personality too.

The mother was completely different. Smartly-dressed, plenty of rings, recent big hairdo, pushy, snobbish. I could tell by the way she looked at me. I had ridden there on my new acquisition, a very loud and totally unreliable Triumph motorbike, so I was carrying a crash helmet. Not the sort of boy she wanted her son to mix with. Her face said it all.

Hartley introduced us, and mentioned that I might be interested in the fishing equipment.

"Well," she said, "You're welcome to it. Just a lot of clutter to me. Show him where it is Tim."

That was it, I was dismissed from the royal presence. I might have been the removal man.

Grandad's house was one of those very big, very old terraced houses in the middle of town. They have four storeys, about eight bedrooms, high ceilings and extensive cellars. Once, many years ago, these were the houses of the professional classes, who had nowadays all moved out to suburban estates and left these old houses to be converted into flats and bedsits. It was sad really; they were beautifully built and very spacious, with polished mahogany banisters, ornate ceiling cornices and an air of vanished grandeur.

Hartley led me down the steps into the cellar. Cellars. There were five rooms just in the basement! Once they were probably used as kitchens or storage rooms, perhaps even for accommodation for the servants. Now there was a room for the washing machine and drier, one for a stack of coal, one for tools and woodwork, one for gardening equipment, and one.... one entirely devoted to fishing. When he opened the door to reveal its delights, I couldn't believe what I was seeing; it was wonderful.

There was everything you could ever need – a whole room full of fishing gear. There were at least a dozen rods, hanging neatly in a rack on the wall as if they were on display in a tackle shop. There were waders, body waders, landing nets, keep nets, rows of fly reels, spinning reels, sea reels, all beautifully organised and set out by someone who really loved his fishing. And these idiots were going to throw it all out!

I just stood there marvelling at the wonderful sight, quite speechless, for I didn't know what to say to him. I couldn't possibly accept any of this - there was thousands of pounds worth of tackle here, an entire lifetime of fishing had been accumulated by a man who loved his sport. And the silly bitch was going to throw it out!

Hartley had sat himself down on a seat, waiting for my reaction. I stared at the seat, an old leather armchair his grandad must have spent many hours in, judging by the shiny patina to the arms.

I didn't know what he was expecting from me, so I played for time. I looked around the room, examining the rods, picking up a reel or two, noting that the tackle was all expensive and in top condition. This was a real fisherman's treasure trove. Not that the scrawny hag with her turkey neck and dangling jewels would appreciate such high quality.

It was then I noticed the bench. So overwhelming had been my first impression of this fabulous angler's den that I hadn't taken notice. A long, stone bench, probably once used for cold storage. Now it was equipped with a fly-tying vice, a spotlight, a magnifying glass on a stand, and best of all, four rows of glass-topped wooden trays containing packets of feathers, all neatly organised, all perfectly labelled in neat copperplate script. There were whole boxes of coloured silks, of peacock herl, of lurex.

I riffled through one of these wooden trays, running my finger along the rows of little packets inside to see what was there. I could hardly contain myself. Each packet contained hackles for use in fly tying. Each one carefully labelled. Each one matched for size. There was a row of cock hackles, a row of hen hackles, another row of cock hackles, slightly bigger this time, then another of larger hen hackles.

This man wasn't just a fisherman; everything was so meticulously presented that his collection had obviously been a labour of love. It would take a lifetime to accumulate a stock of feathers and silks as impressive as this one.

I took out a packet and scanned its contents. A dozen lovely cock hackles in pristine condition. Perfect for creating some Greenwell's Glory.

"What do you think?" asked Hartley.

I was startled at the sound of his voice. I had been so transported to this flyfishing heaven that I had forgotten he was here. He was that sort of boy. Forgettable.

"Your Grandad was certainly a keen fisherman," I said noncommittally.

"He was," said Hartley.

We lapsed into silence.

'Does he have any idea of what a treasure trove he has here?' I wondered. The rods were pure fishing aristocracy, all the best names: Farlows of Pall Mall. Sharpes of Aberdeen. Hardy of Alnwick. The reels were all of the same high quality. Mitchell, Abu, Penn…

There were boxes of colourful floats, of all sizes from tiny quills to great big weighted monsters; there were rows of leads, of fly leaders, of brightly-coloured pike spoons. I couldn't conceal my excitement.

Just when I thought I'd seen everything, Hartley lifted up a wooden box from beneath the bench. I watched as he opened the lid. Inside were dozens of pike plugs – red, blue, yellow, with dangling single trebles, rattling double trebles. I was finding it difficult to keep my composure among this plethora of goodies.

I opened one innocuous little box and it was full of fly lines! New, unused fly lines, floaters, sinktips, weight forward, double tapered! They must have cost a fortune.

I could see that his Grandad had enough tackle here to stock a good-sized fishing shop. I had to grin, for he must have spent a vast amount of time and money on accumulating all this equipment.

There was a clattering of heels on the stairs. It was the mother. She was clearly in a hurry to get me out of the way.

"Well," she said. "What do you think?"

I shrugged. I was embarrassed and didn't know what to say to her.

She was waiting for an answer so the best I could manage was, "He must have been a very dedicated fisherman."

"He was," she snapped. "Fishing was his life. It's all he ever did. Fishing." Her face contorted. "Obsessive he was."

Oh dear, I seemed to have hit a raw nerve there. Odd though how the woman could irritate me so intensely in just a couple of sentences. Someone should tell her not to make those sour faces, the lines were becoming permanent.

"Well, that's it," she said. "Take what you want. It's all going to the tip. I'll be glad to see the back of it. The house goes on the market tomorrow."

'You stupid, stupid woman,' I thought. Ignorance is one thing, but at least she could show the man some respect. This was his entire life's work down here and she was just going to dump the lot.

I picked up a large black and red notebook. It was his fishing diary, neatly written in blue ink. I started to read.

'28th June 1951

An unseasonably cold day did not augur well for our trip to the Tweed, but John and I set off in the Rover in good spirits. John was upset about something, but I trusted he would reveal the reason in good time. Fishing has always calmed the spirits, I have found.'

I shut the diary and put it down. I didn't want to intrude into this poor man's life. He had written personal details in an attractive hand, surely the daughter would want to read it?

"These are quite personal," I said, handing her the book.

She shook her head. "I haven't got time."

I was torn now between two courses of action.

One, I take the lot.

It was worth a fortune. I would never need to buy any fishing tackle ever again. The fly-tying materials alone were worth hundreds of pounds, never mind the rods, the fly lines, the reels.

Two, I tell her how much it is all worth – hundreds, possibly thousands of pounds at auction.

This was a big moral dilemma for a sixteen year old to handle. I looked around the room and lusted for the goodies on show. To take the tackle would give me a lifetime's worth of fishing tackle, so I was sorely tempted, I admit it. Equally I knew that if I did take the tackle I would forever feel guilty, knowing that I had come into such riches by being deceitful.

So should I tell her its true value?

On the other hand, why should I? I'd seen her turn her nose up at me, with my motor cycle helmet and my denim jeans. She was a stupid silly snobbish woman who deserved no sympathy.

And after all, she had just said quite clearly that I was to take it, that she was going to dump the whole lot, so why not rescue the tackle and put it to good use? It would be her own fault.

Hartley was waiting for me to speak. I sensed Mother wanted rid of me, wanted dear Tim to get on with the house clearance.

"What do you think then? Do you want any of it?"

I indicated the trays of fly-tying materials. No doubt they were just old feathers to her.

"I'd like those if that's okay with you."

"Yeah," he said. "That's fine. Glad it's going to a good home."

Mother Hartley said nothing. She just stood there, hands on hips. She stared at me for a few seconds, then, without speaking, turned and left. Her high heels clacked on the stone stairs.

When she was out of hearing, I picked up Grandad's diary and confronted Hartley.

"Hartley," I said, indicating the diary and the room full of fishing equipment, his Grandad's whole sporting life. "Are you sure you don't want to keep any of this?"

He paused, and for a moment there was a glimpse of a personality, but then years of being told what to think by his domineering mother reimposed themselves.

"Mother wants it all to go," he said. "So it goes."

Right. That decided it. I had tried to explain to them, I had turned down the offer of all the tackle. I was taking only what she would no doubt dismiss as a few useless feathers. We gathered the fly-tying materials together, and loaded them into an empty box.

Still I was struck by a feeling of remorse, of responsibility to his old Grandad, of respect for a real fisherman who had dedicated his life to his sport.

"Look, let me pay you something. I can't possibly take all this for nothing."

"What's it worth? A pound?"

A pound! Was he joking?

"That's not much."

"It's fine. Like I said, she just wants rid. It's only going to the tip if you don't take it."

I stood embarrassed for a moment, then shook his hand and took a pound note out of my pocket. "It's a deal."

The pair of us packed up all the boxes of feathers, the vice, the magnifying glass, the light, Grandad's entire fly-tying equipment, and carried it all upstairs.

Mother was waiting by the front door.

"He's taking this," Hartley said, indicating the trays and boxes.

"Good."

Despite my dislike of her, I had an attack of guilty conscience. "Er – Mrs Hartley?"

She glanced up. "Yes? What?"

"Erm – I think maybe you should get Morphets round to value it." (Morphets were the local auctioneers)

She shook her head dismissively.

"No time," she snapped. "I want the place sold."

Fair enough, I thought to myself. I did try to warn her. She wouldn't listen, so be it.

For the last fifty years I have been tying flies with those materials from Grandad Hartley and I'm still catching trout with them. As I had seen from the start, they were really beautiful feathers and silks of the highest quality, and quality lasts, not that she would have known anything about real quality.

Anyway, it has all been my testament to Grandad Hartley, for it was, without doubt, the best quid I've ever spent!

Night fishing

In my experience, night fishing is either tremendously exciting or soporifically boring. There seems to be no middle road between the two extremes. The main trouble for me with night fishing is that it's dark at night and there's not a lot to look at if the fish aren't biting. As a result, you miss one of the great attractions of daytime fishing, the chance to enjoy your surroundings.

If I'm being totally honest, I can think of more interesting ways of spending a night than squatting under a dripping umbrella trying to make out if my neon Dayglo quivertip is starting to quiver. On the positive side, the big advantage of night fishing is that you can sometimes catch bigger and better fish than during the day.

The first time I tried night fishing was one of the most memorable. It was a rare excursion to a private water on the River Ure. The Ure is in the next dale up from my native Nidderdale, and is known on maps as Wensleydale, though old locals still call it Yoredale. It rises high on the fells above Buttertubs Pass, flows down through Hawes, Middleham, Askrigg and Masham as a wonderful trout and grayling fishery. Some of the best fly fishing I have ever had has been on the Ure below Hawes.

Near Ripon the river becomes slower and deeper and is more of a mixed fishery with chunky chub, lunking great eels and belting barbel. Unfortunately most of the Ure is private water (unfortunately, because I'm not a member of any of the clubs which own the rights.)

Luckily for me, I had been invited to share a double ticket by Stanny, my old friend from Junior school days, who was working now as an apprentice lab technician at ICI Fibres in town. For some reason they had fishing tickets open to employees and their guests, and Stan had managed to secure some for the pair of us.

The water was a virtually unfished private stretch near Norton Conyers, which is a stately home and park representing old England at its most historic. The first owners of the house and estate were a Norman family called Conyers, who came to England with William the Conqueror. For centuries the Graham family had been the incumbents of this stately home, and, as Stanny informed me, the current landlord was Sir Richard Graham.

A twisting lane leads off the main Ripon road, winding past willow clumps and thick sedges, through the village of Hutton Conyers and eventually leading to the romantic old park of the Norton Conyers estate.

Charlotte Bronte had visited the house when she was a governess to Mrs Sidgwick, whose parents were then tenants of Norton Conyers. There was a legend in the Graham family that a mad woman had been confined in a room in the attic, a room still known as The Mad Woman's Room, a legend which probably gave Charlotte the idea for the mad Mrs Rochester in *Jane Eyre.*

Here Civil War battles had been a matter of life and death. The squire's Royalist ancestor had ridden home from defeat at the Battle of Marston Moor and so headlong had been his ride, that legend had it he had continued riding up the lane and straight inside the house. He had galloped up the main staircase and so hot had been the horse's iron shoes that he had left a hoofprint burned into the oak steps of the stairs. With the history of the place so interesting, I wondered what the fishing would be like.

Stan had been told that there were massive barbel in this stretch, in shoals which could be seen moving upstream into shallows as darkness descended. Fishing for them in daylight was apparently a waste of time, for they could only be caught at night.

At this stage in my fishing career I hadn't ever caught a

barbel before and dreams of monsters were upon me. Stan had been there once before and insisted that the water was full of huge barbel, but that he had failed to catch any. Apparently they were only catchable at night. As a result of this information, in the days and nights before our trip I wrestled in my dreams with leviathans, denizens of the deep which tugged me from my bed.

I think we were just seventeen, as we drove there in Stanny's prized new possession, an ancient but faithful Morris Minor van. He'd just passed his driving test, so we both had that added air of newly-acquired freedom.

We had with us torches, plenty of grub, and bags full of big barbel-worms (luncheon meat and such exotica being unheard-of in those days.)

We fished all day without seeing a soul. I caught a skinny old trout on a fly, but otherwise the fishing was frankly disappointing. We had seen not a sign of a barbel, nor were there many other fish in evidence. It was obvious that this was wild, untended water.

As a hot afternoon drew on, I tired of fishing and wandered off exploring into the riverbank woods, called Badgerbank and Wilderness Wood, I later discovered. They were real *Toad of Toad Hall* woodlands, wild, untended and full of birds and animals. I imagined the weasels were out there watching me, just waiting for dark when they would pounce.

As darkness began to fall, we returned to the fishing and settled down under steep sandy banks by the side of a large deep pool – one of the few that was relatively free of sunken trees and other obstacles. We spread out our tackle and practised our movements ready for darkness. This done, we finished our sandwiches and lay back to wait for the barbel to appear.

The sun vanished behind hazy trees, the air quickly cooled. Distant sounds – a car on the lane to the big house, a late tractor heading for home - became amplified. Small black creatures fluttered above the pool – bats, not birds, their wing profiles angular and awkward.

The light went slowly.

We had no watches, but an hour or two must have passed in this way. It was very very dark as we were a long way from streetlights. The woods seemed alive with sounds – pigeons bickering, pheasants croaking, the noisy flapping of disturbed ducks. A curlew cackled in faraway fields, then settled down to sleep.

On the water there were no rises, the surface still and grey and apparently empty. Ten yards away I could just about see Stanny curled into his hole in the bank. He waved a white hand. This looked like being a long wait.

I saw them first. Great bow-waves at the tail of the pool.

"Stan!" I called.

A number of large fish were moving upstream, their shoulders almost breaking surface.

"Look at that!"

One, two, four, six - a dozen of them, moving into our pool. It looked like a wolf pack of U boats sliding through the water. There was no doubting now what Stan had been told. These were the biggest river fish either of us had ever seen.

Feverishly, I baited up, my hands suddenly clumsy with haste. 'Slow down,' I told myself. 'You've got all night. Take your time, don't scare them.'

I chose a big tough worm carefully - not one of those fat, thick, soft slow-moving ones, but a thinner, more athletic specimen, one with tough skin, one that squirmed around violently. I threaded him on, as I remembered my Grandad Johnny showing me all those years ago. Right through the worm, then thread him over the barb, carefully up the shank, then pulling the eye through so that he's locked onto the hook. Then once more put the hook through his body. That way the worm hangs naturally, with a little twist – and there's no sign of the hook.

Then to cast, bring the rod back carefully and gently, oh so gently, swing the rod out, releasing quietly so that the weight lands with a soft plop in the middle of the pool and there's no whip or jerk to detach the worm.

It was a cloudy night. Sometimes I could see bright stars, but elsewhere in the sky big black clouds scudded by and covered the light. Now that my eyes had become used to the darkness it was amazing just how much I could see. Certainly, the end of the rod was visible enough, though I checked once with the torch to see that my line was taut. Then I turned it off so as not to scare the fish.

I sat hunched over the rod, my hands tight round the butt. On and on I sat. Somewhere an owl hooted. There were pheasants coughing in the woods. In the distance, maybe miles away, a car pulled away. There were no lights, no houses, nothing human was visible.

All at once I realised the attraction of night fishing. Nature. There was nothing to be afraid of in the dark. Nothing in the natural world could cause me any harm. Only humans caused trouble and there were no humans here, out in the countryside, miles from the nearest village. I thought of all the appalling things which human beings do, of their colossal arrogance and their immense destructiveness, their lack of care for the environment, their greed and the pollution they cause. It seemed a profound revelation – commonplace perhaps, but one that has stuck with me ever since – that in England at least, there is never any need for fear in the dark countryside. The only creature to be feared is man.

I must have lost concentration, someone was calling for me. It was Stan. He sounded excited.

"I think I've got one!"

I began to struggle to my feet.

"Yes, he's on!"

"Do you want a hand?"

"Yes. Bring the net."

Envy of his good fortune mixed with anticipation, for neither of us had even seen a barbel before, let alone caught one. Our only knowledge of them was in the fondly-remembered drawings of *Mr Crabtree Goes Fishing*.

I stumbled up the high bank and ran along to where he was fishing, shimmying down on my backside in my haste to join him, nearly sliding straight down into the black depths.

"Careful!"

"I'm okay. Is he still on?"

"I think so."

At that moment the fish took off on a surging run, the rod bending so fiercely it seemed sure to break.

"Christ, will you look at that!"

There was no need to speak, it was clear Stan was fighting hard just to hold onto the fish. Barbel are the strongest fish in the river, absolute solid muscle, stronger than trout, less dramatic than salmon, but with more dogged determination, longer-lasting than a pike.

This fish was surging up and down the pool, immune

to anything Stanny could do to stop him. It was boring deep down all the time, a potent presence that it seemed we would never even see. Being inexpert barbel anglers, we had no idea of how much pressure could be exerted on the fish without either tugging the hook free or breaking the line.

Stanny let him run and tried to regain line, and in this way he gradually edged him close to us, until the wonderful moment came when he surfaced below us, a white splash in the dark.

I slid the net carefully under him and lifted, almost spilling him out as I underestimated his weight. It took both of us to lift him out. And then there it was – our first sight of a barbel – and what a beauty.

Golden flanked in the torchlight, each scale perfectly-formed and edged with brown. Red fins and a startling white underneath, a heavy fish solid with power. We knelt round him and stared. There was nothing to be said. I just wanted to touch him, but there wasn't time. He was such a magnificent fish we both wanted him back in the water as soon as possible.

We weighed the sagging net.

"Eight pounds."

Stanny gasped. This was the biggest river fish he had ever caught. Then he slid his hands into the water, wet them both, carefully cradled the fish, and knelt by the water to put him back.

The gills pumped twice, the fish flexed his body and with a swish of his tail, vanished from sight.

To say it was a religious experience would be taking things too far, but it was an unforgettable moment, more memorable to me than many supposedly significant moments in my life.

Later in the night I got one too. Seven pounds of golden perfection. It was a thrill just to feel that great strength tugging away on the line – no, not tugging, just pulling with a strength that pound for pound far exceeded my own, a thrill I have never forgotten.

Towards dawn Stanny got another, which was only fair as it was his fishing permit after all, and there's a sense of rough justice in the fishing world, if nowhere else.

We drove home too excited for tiredness, too talkative for sleep. Neither of us would ever forget that moment in the darkness when he called out, "I think I've got one!"

Night fishing for barbel. Unforgettable.

Fishing is an education

Fishing has always had a great deal of influence on the academic performances of my life, and it can be on yours too.

I was, for example, absent from school, fishing at the top of Nidderdale, the day before my critically-important Geography A level examination. There were two ways of looking at this – that fishing was a bad influence which caused me to waste time which could have been more usefully spent in revision (this was my teacher's opinion.) Or that fishing was a beneficial influence, in that the peaceful contemplation I thereby enjoyed enabled me to ignore the rebelliousness and rejection of academia which was all around me in the late Sixties.

While my friends were fighting at the barricades, smoking strange substances and trying to talk like American hippies, I was busily inventing new trout flies and carving pike plugs. In an age of dropouts and breakdowns, at least I survived with my mental faculties intact – which was my opinion, and one I communicated to an irate Headmaster when summoned to his study the following afternoon. He seemed unconvinced. He called me names.

I, however, am quite convinced that fishing helped me to pass the wretched Geography A level examination. I had always found the drudgery of learning such vital information as the production statistics of Brazilian Pig Iron a tedious task, and one unworthy of an intellectual and Kropotkinite rebel such as myself.

I was in the habit of referring scornfully to much of the Geography A level course as 'colouring in maps of Australia' or 'drawing sheep' – a habit which had not endeared me to the Geography master, a humourless individual deeply fascinated by the intricacies of Pig Iron production.

The only part of the course I'd taken any real interest in was the study of river patterns – the different stages in the life cycle of rivers and their effect upon the landscape (and of course on the subsequent fishing stretches which would evolve through time.)

All the other, more studious, A level Geographers spent May 22nd 1967 swotting up Pig Iron Production for the exam next day. I went fishing up Nidderdale and saw Juvenile River Action upon the landscape at first hand (which I suspect was more than the Geography master had ever done.)

Next day, what did I find in the exam, but Question 1: 'Upland Scenery – the effect of rivers in shaping landscapes' – what a doddle! With my comprehensive and very recent knowledge of the subject, I was able to write a stunning answer, one which more than made up for the spurious waffle I wrote about Brazilian Pig Iron.

All this was much to the Geography master's chagrin, as he had gleefully predicted total failure as my best possible mark. When the results came out in August, he was heard to mutter, "I don't believe it!" when he saw my grade A.

I merely said, "It was my drawing of a sheep that did it sir. I bought a new set of coloured crayons especially."

And that was how fishing got me into university.

Back to Ireland

I should have learned my lesson. Fishing had got me into university and I should have stuck with it. Unfortunately I made the big mistake of leaving my roots as a real fisherman behind. Instead of continuing with Geography, in which fishing could play such a vital part, I foolishly listened to others and was seduced by the revolutionary ethos of the time. So, far from taking my crayons and my fishing rods and going off for four years of Geography and Fishing, I had instead applied for Joint Honours in Politics and Social Anthropology.

I chose Politics because I was interested in it. I am less certain of my motives for picking Social Anthropology, not least because I had no idea what Social Anthropology was. I had seen a photograph of some tiny topless females in one of the recommended books, and this may well have influenced my choice, I don't know. Topless photos of anything were pretty hot stuff in Yorkshire in 1967, when bra adverts featured dis-embodied Playtex 'cups' and body shots were banned.

By some strange coincidence, I had elected to go to university in Ireland. I had rejected the thought of studying at the universities of Yorkshire and the North in general as fishing destinations, because I wanted to experiment with fishing in different types of rivers. The University of Reading was nicely on the Thames, but an interview and a Saturday night spent in Reading sent me hot-footing elsewhere. Aberystwyth had been a possibility but reaching Aberystwyth was like trekking through the wastes of Siberia. It took me two days to get there and twice I had got lost, unsuccessfully seeking help from gibbering flat-capped locals who spoke some foreign tongue.

Scotland had tempted me. I liked the fishing and as a

kid had spent many days in the lakes and rivers around Galloway, where my parents sometimes took a caravan. Dumfries, Castle Douglas, and Newton Stewart have some great rivers and lakes but sadly lack a university.

I tried further up the Scottish coast in Argyll, but delightful and unspoiled though it is, again, there was no local university. Edinburgh I considered, but I had to rule it out on the grounds of cost. Edinburgh is one expensive city. In the end, as I explained to my long-suffering dad, it had to be Ireland, the fisherman's paradise.

Ireland in those days was still full of free fishing and cheap accommodation, so I could hardly wait to start the next stage of my academic development. I took all my tackle, including rods, waders, fly boxes and even a couple of pens in case I had to do any writing at university, and I was all set up. Four years at Queen's University Belfast, with fabulous fishing only a short trip away in all directions.

Social Anthropology turned out to studying little people. To be exact, tiny topless little people. Specifically, tribes of pygmies in Borneo. No doubt wonderful people in their own small way, but not terribly interesting to a seventeen-year-old just released from six years' incarceration in a remote Yorkshire boarding school.

Furthermore, never having been fishing to Borneo, I knew nothing about the place – a distinct handicap to someone who had hoped to gain an Honours degree in much the same manner as he had gained his Geography A level.

Politics was even less interesting. There weren't even tiny topless titties to liven up Politics. I had, foolishly, thought it might be something actually to do with Politics -

the Machiavellian cut and thrust of our attempts at governing ourselves, perhaps even the struggle for democracy, the fight against Fascism, the threat of Communism, even the role of the Anarchist…

Not a bit of it. It was four years' study of American Social Administration and Systems.

Yes, exactly my sentiments. And the books about it which they fondly expected me to buy and read… have you ever read any American academic works? Verbal claptrap. Latinate, verbose, unintelligible, taking hours of convoluted prose to say the simplest things.

I hated it.

By now at the age of seventeen I was developing my political philosophy into becoming a dedicated Bakuninite revolutionary, with occasional traces of my old favourite, Kropotkinism, though I sometimes hankered after the revolutionary teachings of Marx, Engels and Dennis the Menace.

I was not in the mood for the tedious American propaganda being spouted at me by the lecturers. To me America was capitalism written large, a society devoted to greed, corruption and materialism. I understood now why the only internationally-known products of American culture at the time were Yogi Bear and BooBoo.

I decided I would head for the riverbank.

Strangford

After only a couple of weeks of university, and tiring of Politics and the little people, four of us absconded for the day to the countryside. I had quickly made friends on the course with a fellow Englishman, a Geordie called Peter, someone like me devoted to fun and frolics rather than American institutions, though not, sadly, a fisherman.

Peter had a car, an ancient and incredibly rusty and untaxed Sunbeam Rapier, so with two other escapees from American Administration we piled in one afternoon and headed out of the city. Fortified by several pints in the Errigal we headed up the Newtownards Road towards the countryside. Delighted to be free of academic life, we burst into song and all the way out of the city we sang '*My Green Tambourine*' at the tops of our voices.

At the Ring Road there were baffling signs pointing in all directions. It was all very confusing. We had no map, no idea where to go, and we were all pissed so we didn't really care where we went anyway. After a brief discussion along the lines of, "Where should we go?"

"Who gives a toss?"

"Oh it's too bright, turn off that sun!"

we did six laps of the roundabout and headed for Donaghadee, which I knew from my childhood to be a pretty little seaside town. Our plan was now to go for a swim.

I was aware that Peter and the other two were looking for fun, preferably involving much more drinking and hopefully meeting some women, and while I was not averse to either, I was primarily looking for somewhere to go fishing. I was missing it so much. I wanted rivers and loughs.

We had no idea where to find any of these necessities, but wove our winding way south. Unfortunately in our meanderings we somehow missed Donaghadee and the entire Irish Sea coastline, instead finding ourselves heading inland on the road to Dublin. No-one seemed to mind, and we continued south on the general principle that south was warmer than north. I was quite pleased as the rivers and loughs I so craved were not to be found at the seaside.

We ended up in an attractive little town called Strangford. We got out of the car, marvelling at the beauty of the place. We were still quite pissed and Strangford seemed very bright as we stood there shielding our eyes on a vivid green hillside overlooking the water.

Strangford was a pretty little town of colourfully-painted cottages and a pub or two, on one shore of Strangford Lough, a huge sea lough and the largest in the United Kingdom. The lough was immense, looking like an inland sea, stretching miles and miles inland most of the way back to Belfast, while to our right, the other end of the lough fed through a narrow channel and led at great speed into the Irish Sea. It was an idyllic scene, one in which I felt immediately at peace. I could just imagine living here, and having a little boat, fishing and sailing on this inland sea.

Just to compound our impressions that we had somehow landed in paradise, the sky was blue and cloudless, the air fresh and salty.

From across the little bay there came a noisy banging sound, and we watched as an oddly-shaped little ferry slid its way from the Strangford jetty to do battle with the strong currents of the lough, conveying a couple of cars and a handful of passengers to the village on the other side. The current was so powerful the little ferry had to edge its mazy way across the lough, like an uncertain crab. It looked so funny that it somehow encapsulated the attractiveness of the whole scene.

"Great this, isn't it?" said Peter.

"Yep." I was too stunned by the setting to speak in more than monosyllables, though six pints of Guinness on an empty stomach hadn't helped develop my vocabulary.

We stood and watched in silent admiration at the unspoilt beauty of the scenery.

Peter then spoke those fateful words, words that were to change my life.

"D'you know Cluffy boy, I could live here," he said quietly.

This was just what I was thinking. Belfast had its attractions – mostly hundreds of stunning-looking girls – but this place was picture perfect and there were sure to be girls here somewhere.

A fatefully bright idea occurred to me. It was like seeing "STRIKE PETER, STRIKE!" in the sky from *Mr Crabtree Goes Fishing.*

I tugged at Peter's arm excitedly. "Bloody brilliant idea!"

"What?"

"Living here!"

He shook his head regretfully. "No. We can't."

"Why not?"

"Cos it's thirty miles from the university."

This temporarily quietened our enthusiasm. We stood in silence. The other two had wandered off in search of alcohol and women.

We could see some little sailing dinghies milling about in a bay below us. I remembered now that I had always wanted to sail.

"Be good though, wouldn't it?"

It would indeed, but there were our academic studies to consider. After all, we were supposed to be working hard for a degree. The authorities at Queen's might not like it if we absconded to Strangford and spent our days fishing and sailing and wandering the woods and chasing women and drinking in the evening. Admittedly, we only had about two lectures a week, and we'd already given up on attending these. There were tutorials to consider, though sadly we'd already missed a few of those as well.

Peter must have been thinking along the same lines.

"We could always go back to Queen's for the occasional tutorial, just to keep them happy."

I brightened at this.

"And it's odds-on they won't notice if we're missing a lecture or two."

"Now that's a thought."

Silence descended on us once more. The little sailing dinghies were milling about in close formation, obviously having a race of some sort. I wondered what the river fishing was like, and there were certain to be plenty of loughs around here somewhere.

I think it was me that made the fatal, final decision.

"Well, why don't we?"

"Don't we what?"

"Live here."

Once again, conversation stalled. The Irish Sea was visible just beyond the bay at the end of the lough. I remembered fishing with my dad and brother at Bangor and Donaghadee. We had gone out in a boat to the Copeland Islands and caught a boatful of fish that day. If we lived at Strangford we could dine on the fresh fish we caught and save money. It was another compelling idea.

"We could live here full time. Go back to Queen's for the occasional tutorial like you said. Maybe even an odd lecture or two."

It was an insane suggestion, but such was the powerful attraction of Strangford, we decided there and then that this was what we would do.

And so we did.

In the pub - or was it in the pubs - of Strangford that afternoon and evening everyone we met was very friendly, and though none of the people we met were attractive seventeen year old girls we were confirmed in our opinion that by great good fortune we had blundered into somewhere very special.

We met, in rapid order: a man who offered to take us sailing, a man who offered to sell us a sailing boat for only £100 (which we instantly accepted); a man who bought us a round of drinks, and best of all, a man who knew of a cottage to rent.

Shortly afterwards we were out in the open air, on a hillside overlooking the lough. A man was showing us round a cottage, an idyllic Gothic cottage, the gate lodge to a stately home. He was talking away as he was a very friendly man, but we weren't listening. We didn't need to. We were sold on the place from the moment we set eyes on it.

For ten shillings a week (50p) Peter and I rented the cottage. It had everything we needed - an open fire, a rudimentary kitchen, and space for several of us to sleep. It was surrounded by woods, and a lane led down through these woods to Strangford Lough itself. There was a little bay, a beach and unbelievably, the rent also included the use of a rowing boat, tied up at the nearby jetty.

The very next day I quit my Belfast lodgings, packed up my clothes, my fishing tackle and both my pens and some paper and joined Peter in the rusty Rapier.

I was going fishing again. It was to be the next chapter of my fishing life.

About the Author

David Clough is a born and bred Yorkshireman, though he has occasionally ventured out of God's Own County on fishing expeditions. He is intensely proud of his county, its rich and proud history and its wonderful people. His interests apart from fishing are writing, cricket, sport and history.

He is the author of award-winning short stories and was for a time Associate Writer at the Royal Court Theatre in London.

Available worldwide from Amazon

www.mtp.agency

www.facebook.com/mtp.agency

@mtp_agency

Printed in Great Britain
by Amazon